*This is a thoughtful and extremely practical look at one of the most important features of local church life. Both new Christians and mature Christians could read it with real profit. Bread and wine will take on a much greater significance when we apply the lessons spelt out in the book.*

Steve Gaukroger

*It is surely a cause for great joy to witness a renewed emphasis upon, and a proper Scriptural understanding of the Eucharist in many of the Reformed and Protestant traditions today. Steve Motyer gives us a vision of what dimensions such a renewed eucharistic vision might have for all Christians.*

Rt. Revd. Michael Marshall

Remember Jesus *is both biblical and practical. My mind was enlightened, my heart warmed, and I was helped to a new appreciation of the place of the Lord's Supper in the life of the Church and of the Christian.*

Colin Sinclair

# Remember Jesus

A Users' Guide to Understanding and
Enjoying Holy Communion

## Steve Motyer

Christian Focus Publications

ISBN 1-85792-153-4

Published by
Christian Focus Publications Ltd.
Geanies House, Fearn, Ross-shire,
IV20 1TW, Scotland, Great Britain

Printed and bound in Great Britain by
Cox & Wyman Ltd, Reading, Berkshire

Cover design by Donna Macleod

# Contents

# Foreword

There seems to be a widespread and welcome readiness today to reconsider those different understandings of the Eucharist which have traditionally divided churches from each other. Steve Motyer's book *Remember Jesus* makes an excellent contribution to the debate. Its value is out of all proportion to its size.

It is a fine combination of theory and practice, ideals and reality, history and theology, doctrine and devotion. It is well informed and persuasively argued. The author seems to be equally at home in the Old and New Testaments, the Fathers and the Reformers, and modern Catholic and Protestant scholars as well. Yet he wears his learning lightly. He spares us footnotes. He writes clearly and compellingly. His approach is user-friendly.

Above all, Steve Motyer's treatment of the Lord's Supper is fresh and even innovative. He offers the churches a way forward, solidly based on a biblical understanding. His collection of Communion hymns, old and new, makes a fitting climax.

No thoughtful Christian, whatever his or her church background, could fail to be illumined and challenged by reading *Remember Jesus*.

*John Stott*

# 1. Setting the scene

This book is meant to be useful to Christians of all sorts. It is simply meant to answer two vital questions:

* What is this thing called the Holy Communion / Eucharist / Sacrament / Mass / Breaking of Bread / Lord's Supper?

and

* How can I get the most out of it when I take part?

It is written for Christians of all churches who want to understand. The vast majority of Christians belong to churches which lay great emphasis on this service of eating and drinking. Only the Quakers, the Salvation Army and some of the new house churches do not celebrate it. But what is it? Why do we do it? Why do the churches differ so much in the way they do it? And when we do it, how can we make sure we are doing it properly?

Its celebration is amazingly varied throughout the Christian church. Dom Gregory Dix, an Anglican monk who published a most influential book on it in 1945, summed it up like this in a famous passage:

Was there ever another command so obeyed? For century after century, spreading slowly to every continent and country and among every race on earth, this action has been done, in every conceivable human circumstance, for every conceivable human need from infancy and before it to extreme old age and after it, from the pinnacles of earthly greatness to the refuge of fugitives in the caves and dens of the earth. Men have found no better thing than this to do for kings at their crowning and for criminals going to the scaffold; for armies in triumph or for a bride and bridegroom in a little country church; for the proclamation of a dogma or for a good crop of wheat; for the wisdom of the Parliament of a mighty nation, or for a sick old woman afraid to die .... The sheer stupendous quantity of the love of God which this ever repeated action has drawn from the obscure Christian multitudes through the centuries is in itself an overwhelming thought.

Yes, it is the most distinctive act of Christian worship. It stood out to the pagans who met the first Christians in Rome and immediately accused them of cannibalism. For centuries it was known as the 'holy mystery', the special rite at the heart of the Christian life from which all unbelievers were barred.

And yet many Christians, I believe, live with a

vague sense of puzzlement or even of guilt towards
it. They cannot quite see why it should have the
importance their church obviously attaches to it.
Others put their minds into neutral when they
participate. It means a lot to them, but at a deep level
beyond rational thought. If asked to put into words
of their own what was going on, they would be a bit
stuck! What matters is the occasion, the actions, the
words, the atmosphere, the feel of being close to
God.

If you are like that, this book is for you! It has
three parts:

*Part One* looks at the questions surrounding the
Eucharist (that's the name I am going to use for
convenience in this book. It is also the most ancient
name) – and at the differences between the churches
and the reasons for them. We will start from the
questions that people ask.

*Part Two* looks at the teaching of the Bible about
the Eucharist. If we come to the Bible with the
questions of Part One in mind, then I believe that we
will be able to find some very helpful answers. In
this section (and indeed throughout), the transla-
tions of Bible passages are my own.

*Part Three* is then a practical guide to participating in the Eucharist. It is meant to help worshippers
make the most of joining in.

If you want to, you can jump straight to Part
Three, although the practical suggestions there
come out of the thoughts about the Eucharist in Part

Two. You can also jump straight to Part Two – although our study of the biblical teaching is designed to answer the questions that come out of Part One.

One preliminary comment. In Part One I refer frequently to the Reformation. This was the notable revival of the church which took place in the sixteenth century, starting in Germany under the leadership of Martin Luther, and then spreading to the rest of Europe. We cannot ignore it, because one of the central issues in the Reformation was the understanding of the Eucharist. Putting it simply, the Reformers rejected the view which had been taught by the Roman Catholic church for centuries, and the result – eventually – was the formation of the many 'Protestant' churches we see around us today (Lutheran, Anglican, Reformed, Presbyterian, Baptist and their many off-shoots). So the interpretation of the Eucharist is foundational for all the churches. There would not be so many 'varieties' today if this sixteenth-century debate had not taken place.

In Part One I focus on the life and writings of Nicholas Ridley, a Reformer particularly dear to me, because he first encountered the dangerous new thinking from the Continent while studying and teaching at the College where I arrived to study exactly 450 years after him! I would like to dedicate this book to his memory: a brave, wise and godly man who never let controversy compromise his gentleness of spirit and who lived and died by the Word of God.

I also want to pay tribute to my dear father, Alec Motyer. So far as I can remember, it was he who first mentioned to me the stimulating thought about prophetic signs developed in chapter 9. And if this book is a blessing to anyone, it will be due in no small part to his prayers for it. In the final chapter I have included some of his lovely Communion hymns, previously unpublished.

I am grateful too to friends and colleagues at London Bible College for suggesting hymns for inclusion in that chapter, and also to John Stott – not only for contributing his generous foreword, but also for making some most helpful comments. Dr Nelson Kraybill kindly helped me with information about the Mennonites and early Baptists.

I also want to express my gratitude to the various copyright holders who gave me permission to include some recently-published hymns in chapter 16, and in particular to Bishop Timothy Dudley-Smith for his kindness and generosity (and also of course for his hymns!).

I hope that you enjoy reading this book as much as I have enjoyed researching and writing it!

# Part One:
# Questions and Quarrels

What are the things that puzzle people about the Eucharist? I suppose we should not be surprised that they are the same things that have always puzzled people. If only they had remained as questions, and not also become quarrels! Actually the questions are of two types. There are

* *practical questions* to do with how we actually administer or receive the Eucharist. Why do the churches all differ so much over it? Must there be a priest or minister in charge? Do we have to be in a 'proper' spiritual state to receive – and if so, how do we get into it? Who is allowed to receive? How often should we do it? These practical questions cannot be separated from

* *theoretical questions* about the nature and meaning of the Eucharist. What is it? Why did Jesus institute it? What actually happens to the bread and wine? How do they bring God's blessing to us?

In this first part we will tackle these two sorts of questions together. A glance at the Contents page will reveal the journey ahead. But we will not be seeking answers so much as clarifying the questions, by looking at the differences between the churches and exploring the reasons for them. Then in Part Two we will begin to look for answers, as we turn to the Bible.

# 2. A meal that unites?

On 16th October 1555, two Bishops of the Church of England were led into the sunshine outside Balliol College in Oxford, and tied with a chain to a wooden stake. Dry sticks and gunpowder were placed around them, and the fire started. As it began to burn, Bishop Latimer called to Bishop Ridley, 'Be of good comfort, Master Ridley, and play the man. We shall this day light such a candle, by God's grace, in England, as I trust shall never be put out!'

Hugh Latimer died quickly, because he was old and frail. But the fire did not take well around Nicholas Ridley, Bishop of London and former Master of Pembroke College, Cambridge. In agony he cried to God and suffered for a long time, until finally the flames reached the gunpowder. In a moving tribute the poet William Wordsworth wrote of their death, 'Earth never witnessed object more sublime In constancy, in fellowship more fair!'

Why did this happen? It took place because Ridley and Latimer had changed their views about the Eucharist, and now held the dangerous 'new' opinions which had been imported from the Reformation in Germany. They had been in prison for over two years, and had been condemned following a big 'disputation' on the subject in Oxford the previous April.

It seems amazing to us now that Christians could do this to each other over their understanding of the Eucharist. One of the best books written recently on the Eucharist is by Donald Bridge and David Phypers, called *The Meal That Unites?*. I imagine that they wish they could have left the question-mark off the title. But sadly the Eucharist, which is meant to express the unity of the body of Christ with the Lord our Head, has actually been a cause of disunity throughout the history of the church. This goes right back to the beginning: as we shall see, Paul's deep teaching on it was given in response to the disunity of the church in Corinth. When they came together for the Lord's Supper (1 Cor. 11:20), the Corinthian church simply managed to reinforce their divisions.

But Donald Bridge and David Phypers symbol-ise something new. One is a Baptist minister, and the other an Anglican trained in the Catholic tradi-tion. Their book illustrates a remarkable new 'com-ing together' on the Eucharist – something that has been happening quietly over the last forty years, and something that would have amazed previous generations of Christians. The wounds of centuries are slowly being healed. A spirit of trust and co-operation has replaced suspicion and hostility. There is not yet agreement: the churches as a whole have not yet committed themselves to an agreed statement on the meaning of the Eucharist, nor to a fully common pattern or service of celebration. But there is a surprising measure of common ground. For instance, Anglicans or Episcopalians attending a Catholic Eucharist may come away feeling that they have hardly left home. In recent years the United Reformed Church, the Methodists and the Baptists have all published prayer-books and services which draw quite heavily on the new Anglican and Catholic services – believe it or not!

This new 'coming together' needs to be handled carefully. In the past, much blood (literally) has been spilled over the disagreements we are going to survey in this part of the book. Christians have fought each other, imprisoned and tortured each other, burned each other alive, regarded each other as spawn of the Devil because of disagreements over the Eucharist. Indeed, even to call it 'the Eucharist' as opposed to 'the Lord's Supper' was until recently to wave a flag which put you in one camp and separated you from others. Just because there has been so much disagreement, we need to be really careful in our own handling of the issues. We cannot simply write off the passions of our forefathers in the faith as misguided enthusiasm. What motivated them? Why did they feel so strongly? Should we imitate their passion today?

At rock bottom, what motivated them all was *concern for truth*. This was the case, whatever side they were on. For instance, Ridley wrote shortly

before he died a 'Brief Declaration' in which he
summed up the debate and his views. He begins it
with a prayer:

> Therefore our heavenly Father, the author and
> fountain of all truth, the bottomless sea of all
> understanding, send down we beseech thee, thy
> Holy Spirit into our hearts, and lighten our
> understanding with the beams of thy heavenly
> grace.

He was convinced that the truth could only be
found in God's Word. He wrote, 'My mind is and
ever shall be (God willing) to set forth sincerely the
true sense and meaning (to the best of my understanding) of God's most holy Word, and not to
decline from the same, either for fear of worldly
danger, or else for hope of gain.' And in that spirit
he faced martyrdom.

On the other hand, the charge on which he was
executed was that he 'stubbornly defended certain
opinions contrary to the Word of God and the
received faith of the church'. His opponents were
also concerned to maintain scriptural truth and
practice.

Of course there were mixed motives, and all
kinds of dreadful abuses of fellowship and Christian love. But basically on all sides there was a deep
concern for truth and for obedience to God's Word.
These fierce debates took place in an age when

concern for truth could lead to dreadful abuses of power. Bishop Ridley himself, six years before he died, took part in the examination of Joan Bocher, one of the earliest Baptists. The issues in her case were different (they concerned her views about the virgin birth). Ridley did his best to persuade her to change her mind, visiting her regularly with Thomas Cranmer, the Archbishop of Canterbury. But when she refused to change, he and Cranmer supported her execution.

Thank God we do not behave towards each other in this way still! But we will not do justice to our past if we simply forget the passions that created the distinct churches to which we belong. We too must have a deep concern for truth, and for the teaching of the Scriptures. That is why this book has its particular shape! First we look at our questions and quarrels, then we turn for help to the Scriptures.

Of course, that does not solve everything, as the example of Nicholas Ridley shows. Both he and his opponents believed that the Scriptures supported their viewpoint. In the long run, we may find that we have to continue to differ. But let us do so after the deepest possible thought – and with the deepest possible love. Concern for love and for truth: truth on which to build our own lives, love on which to build fellowship with those who view things differently. That's the Christian way! And together with both – a willingness to look afresh at the Scriptures, and if necessary to be led by them to dangerous 'new' opinions just as Ridley was.

It is fascinating to see how the questions which people ask about the Eucharist match the debates which have raged (literally) in centuries gone by. In the next four chapters we will think about these questions.

# 3. Who may take Communion?

It is amazing how much heartache this one simple question has caused – and still causes. People often question whether they are worthy to participate – especially Christians who take seriously Paul's warning in 1 Corinthians 11:27, 'whoever eats the bread or drinks the cup of the Lord in an unworthy manner will be guilty of sinning against the body and blood of the Lord'.

The question, 'How can I be sure that I will partake worthily?' has particularly vexed Christians in the Presbyterian tradition. In this tradition there are often no more than four Eucharists per year, sometimes only two, and great emphasis is laid on proper preparation. Celebrations were (and are) preceded by an address 'fencing the table', that is, inviting worthy participants and warning the unworthy.

For instance, Robert Murray McCheyne, the great minister of St Peter's Dundee in the 1830s, includes a note in his journal about the 'communion season' held there in April 1838: 'I fenced the tables from Christ's eyes of flame'. That is, he gave an address on Revelation 1:14, 'his eyes were like blazing fire', presumably reminding people that

Christ could see the inmost thoughts of their hearts
so that they could conceal no impure or unworthy
motives from him. It is not surprising that many felt
hesitant about participation!

Most churches have a system of formal admission to the Eucharist. In the Lutheran, Anglican
(Episcopalian) and Catholic churches it is linked to
confirmation, in which candidates publicly affirm
their faith in front of the congregation. Confirmation is usually preceded by a course of instruction.
But beyond this there is little emphasis, nowadays,
on personal preparation for the Eucharist or on the
dangers of unworthy participation. Similarly, Baptist churches have on the whole been quite relaxed
about who may participate. Participants must of
course be believers, and therefore will have been
baptised. But apart from this no searching questions will be asked prior to admission.

The Eastern Orthodox churches are even more
relaxed. They allow baptised children to take Communion from infancy. They believe that, if it is right
to baptise infants, then they should be admitted to
Communion also. The Church of England is currently debating whether Christian children should
be admitted to Communion prior to their confirmation.

Probably the other churches have something to
learn from the seriousness of the Presbyterians
here. We will think in Part Two about the meaning
of Paul's warning words in 1 Corinthians 11:27.

What does it mean to 'sin against the body and blood of the Lord'? Whatever Paul means, it cannot be right to ignore him!

On the other hand, some churches have limited participation deliberately. Before the Second Vatican Council, Catholics would usually only take the bread. The wine would not be administered, for fear that drops of it might fall on the floor. This limitation has largely now been lifted in the Catholic church. For very different reasons, Strict Baptists and Brethren churches have traditionally limited participation to the baptised members of each congregation. Visitors would not be permitted to participate, unless they brought a letter from their home church confirming their membership there. So generally speaking, visitors from other denominations would not be allowed to participate at all.

Similarly, non-Catholics are not allowed to take Communion in Catholic Churches, nor are Catholics allowed to do so in non-Catholic churches. In most other churches, visitors are admitted to Communion without question, although in some Presbyterian churches intending participants must obtain a token in advance.

Churches also differ greatly over the preparation they demand. We will touch on this in Part Three, below. Generally, the churches with infrequent Communion require more preparation than those in which Communion is celebrated monthly or weekly.

Where is right and wrong in all this? In Part Two some answers will emerge as we look again at the Scriptures. And in Part Three we will also think about some practical issues of hygiene which might sometimes mean restricting access to the cup.

# 4. How often should we take Communion?

Here again there is great variation between the churches. Some traditions commend a daily Eucharist – especially for priests, monks and nuns in the Roman Catholic tradition. For others a weekly communion is the approved pattern. Here we can think especially of the Roman Catholic and Anglican churches, which recommend this pattern to their members. This is actually something comparatively new for the Church of England. The so-called 'Oxford Movement' in the nineteenth century led to a widespread restoration of weekly Communion as part of its attempt to re-introduce Catholic practices into the English-speaking church. This movement deeply affected all the Anglican churches worldwide.

In fact, however, evangelicals within the Church of England had long been encouraging more frequent communion than the three times a year which was the general norm (at Christmas, Easter and Pentecost). This was one of the features of the early Methodists, under the leadership of John and Charles Wesley, who held a very high view of the impor-

tance of the Eucharist. They encouraged their con-
verts to attend Communion weekly if possible, at
their local Parish church.

Brethren churches still regard the weekly 'breaking of bread' as their central act of worship. This
has been their most consistent and distinctive feature since their beginning in the 1830's.

In Presbyterian churches the tradition is more
infrequent. Communion 'seasons' are usually held
four times a year, sometimes only twice a year. But
this comparative infrequency has led to greater
emphasis on careful participation and preparation –
and has produced some wonderful hymns. Communion 'seasons', sometimes with thousands of
worshippers gathering from a wide area, have been
spiritual mountain-top experiences for many, just
because they do not happen frequently. Similarly in
the Orthodox churches the usual practice is to take
Communion just four or five times a year.

In the Lutheran and Reformed churches, with
their strong traditional emphasis on the ministry of
the Word, monthly celebration is the norm. And
this is the case too for most Baptist, Pentecostal and
free evangelical churches, where a Eucharist is
often attached to a 'standard' morning service, or
possibly incorporated into it as an addition to the
usual programme. But there is much local variation
here. The great Baptist leader and preacher Charles
Haddon Spurgeon, for instance, strongly
commended weekly communion.

There is no standard pattern! Experience counts for a lot here. *Each of us needs, if possible, to conform happily to the tradition of the church to which we belong, and to live within and benefit from that tradition.* In Part Two we will ask whether the Scriptures give us any hints about frequency.

# 5. Does there have to be a 'priest' in charge of the service?

Over this issue there has been deep disagreement through the centuries – and there still is today. As a country Vicar in the Church of England, I encountered the strongly-held conviction that it would be wrong if anyone other than a priest stepped behind the altar-rails to lead the service or administer the bread and wine. Yes!, the answer would be: there must be a 'priest' in charge, because somehow the service will not be a 'proper' Eucharist unless priestly hands perform it.

What lies behind this view, now held instinctively by many? The issue concerns *validity*. Way back in the early church, when various sectarian groups began to emerge with strange ideas, the issue of the validity of their worship was high on the agenda. Was it valid Christian worship? If so, then there could be no justification for expelling them or withholding fellowship. At first, this issue was not separated from the other, even more vital question, Are their views right or wrong – orthodox or unchristian, Scriptural or not? Determining this would mean a laborious process of examination.

But as time went on this process was short-circuited. It was easier to start at the other end and ask, Have they separated themselves off from the mainline, orthodox church? Are they living as sects? If the answer to this was 'Yes', then they could be regarded as unchristian, whatever their actual teaching was. The test of orthodoxy thus became formal, rather than doctrinal: not 'What do they believe?', but 'Do they still regard themselves as belonging to the one true Catholic church?'

Most sectarian groups started life as the followers of a single charismatic leader, often one whose ministry was not authorised by the church. So the formal authorisation of ministry came to be regarded as the vital test of the validity of doctrine, and also of worship. This happened quite early on. It was Cyprian in the fourth century who left us with the famous saying (in Latin), 'extra ecclesiam nulla salus', 'there is no salvation outside the church!' This means: unless you belong to the one true Catholic and apostolic church, you cannot be saved, and you cannot therefore engage in Christian worship. And how is membership of the one true Catholic church defined and shown? By its *ministry*.

So at first this emphasis on the authorisation of the ministry was meant to safeguard the purity of teaching in the church. Authorised ministers were authorised to teach, as well as to celebrate the sacraments and lead worship. But eventually the emphasis on safeguarding the truth faded, and the emphasis on priestly administration of the sacraments became all-important. In time an almost magical view of the priesthood developed, along with a magical view of the Eucharist. To perform it could cure ill health, grant success in war, guarantee good weather and crops, give safety in journeying ... and knock years off purgatory.

For a while my family and I worshipped at St Mary's North Mymms in Hertfordshire, England, where the oldest part of the building is a 'chantry chapel' built in the 14th century. England was covered with such chapels in Mediaeval times. In this case, it was built under the will of William de Kestevene, who died in 1361, and provided money not only for the chapel but also to pay for a priest who lived on the spot and said Mass daily for William's soul. He hoped to reduce the time he had to spend in purgatory before going to heaven.

This magical view of the Mass persisted until modern times – and is still alive and well in some parts of the Roman Catholic Church. It is satirised by Robert Browning in his poem 'The Bishop orders his tomb at St Praxted's Church', where the bishop says,

> And then how I shall lie through centuries,
> And hear the blessed mutter of the Mass,
> And see God made and eaten all day long,
> And feel the steady candle-flame, and taste
> Good strong thick stupefying incense-smoke!

So priestly presidency at the Eucharist moved a long way from its original reason – safeguarding the purity of teaching in the church. We might have expected the Reformation to change it: after all, one of the reasons for the Reformation was opposition to the oppressive clericalism of the Roman Catholic Church, and one of the central new doctrines was 'the priesthood of all believers'. But only the Baptists introduced 'lay' celebration, that is, permitted any member of the congregation to lead the Eucharist.

The reason is not hard to find: the original purpose of the restriction re-appeared! One of the central principles on which the Reformers insisted was the unity of Word and sacrament – that is, they wanted to reintroduce the reading of the Scriptures and preaching into the celebration of the Eucharist. The Eucharist could not be a stand-alone. It had to take its place within the wider worship of the congregation, which (they insisted) must centre on the Scriptures. Into whose hands could this ministry of the Word be entrusted? There would have to be an authorised minister, who could be trusted to teach the truth, the whole truth, and nothing but the truth.

But in time many Protestant churches – of all types, Anglican, Lutheran, Presbyterian, even Baptist – became just as 'clerical' as the Roman Catholic Church before the Reformation. Hence the feeling I encountered as an Anglican Vicar!

The dear folk I was seeking to serve would have been horrified by the views of the early Plymouth Brethren. The Brethren owe their origin to the energetic ministry of John Nelson Darby, an Irish Anglican clergyman who became increasingly disillusioned with the national church, and eventually left it (in 1833), rejecting the whole idea of a priestly 'caste' and emphasising the uniting power of the Eucharist (or the 'breaking of bread', as the Brethren preferred to call it). The church is no hierarchical organisation, but a brotherhood, held together and defined by the Supper it eats with the Lord. So the Brethren ordained no ministers, although the Eucharist was (and is) absolutely central in their worship. Their answer to the question at the head of this chapter was 'Certainly not!'. To appoint a 'priest', they thought, would be a denial of the gospel, a violation of the unity of the body of Christ and a dishonour to the Lord who is the only Mediator between God and humankind. They held together Word and sacrament by allowing anyone to minister either, just as the Spirit led the gathering of the Lord's people.

So – do we need a 'priest' in order validly to celebrate the Eucharist? If we look at the example of the Brethren, then we must answer 'No' – unless we feel inclined to discount their Christian experience altogether. Of course the consistent Roman Catholic position – still officially held by the Vatican – is that all non-Catholic worship is invalid because it takes place 'extra ecclesiam' as Cyprian put it, 'outside the church'. But if we follow the Brethren example and allow a free-for-all, do we endanger true teaching, order and discipline within the church?

Again, Part Two will supply some answers as we turn to the Scriptures.

# 6. What actually happens to the bread and the wine?

This is the central question fought over at the time of the Reformation. For his 'new' views here, Ridley and many fellow-Reformers were executed. And it still puzzles people today, although most people are content not to ask the kind of precise questions which were fired at Ridley during his trial. In fact, many find it hard to imagine how opinions could be so strongly held that rivals would want to kill each other.

The way services are conducted in many churches conveys the general impression that something special happens to the bread and the wine. They are treated in ways very different from 'ordinary' bread and wine – set apart on a table, prayed over, solemnly broken, distributed in very small quantities, with the remainder reverently consumed at the end of the service. In some churches the celebrant will lift them above his head, kneel before them, and carefully wash his fingers before and after handling them.

Alongside these actions, the words of the service sometimes convey the idea that in some sense the bread and wine become identified with the body and blood of Christ. The actual words used vary enormously from church to church, but in nearly all churches the words of Jesus from the story of the institution of the Lord's Supper are read, 'This is my body ... this is my blood'.

In many churches these words will be applied to the bread and wine with a prayer like the one used in the British Anglican Alternative Service Book: 'Grant that by the power of your Holy Spirit these gifts of bread and wine may be to us his body and his blood'. The German Lutheran prayer says similarly, 'send down upon us the Holy Spirit ... and grant that under this bread and wine we receive in true faith the very body and blood of your Son to our salvation'. In the Prayer Book of the American Episcopal Church the celebrant prays over the bread and wine, 'sanctify them by your Holy Spirit to be the Body and Blood of Jesus Christ our Lord'.

Is it worth asking in what sense the bread and wine 'become' or 'are' the body and blood of Christ? Most Christians are content, I believe, just to retain a general impression and to believe that eating and drinking in this way does them spiritual good. Many churches – for instance, the Brethren and the Baptists – have never sought to define it more exactly, even though (in the case of the Brethren) the Eucharist has been so central in their worship.

If Christians had not tried to answer the question, 'Exactly in what sense is Christ present in the Eucharist?', it would honestly have been much better for the church as a whole. But we human beings are incurably curious, and cannot help asking questions like that. And actually it is enormously helpful to pursue such a question through the Scriptures. If only it had not caused such division in the church!

In order to set out the various views it is helpful to go back to Bishop Ridley and listen to the charges laid against him at his trial. They were that he 'stubbornly defended certain opinions contrary to the Word of God and the received faith of the church, as in denying the true and natural body of Christ and his natural Blood to be in the Sacrament of the altar; secondarily in affirming the substance of bread and wine to remain after the words of consecration; and thirdly in denying the Mass to be a lively sacrifice of the Church for the quick and the dead'. Three points are made here, which need a little explanation.

(1) Ridley and the Reformers rejected the view of the Roman Catholic Church that the bread and wine *really* become the body and blood of Christ. At the Last Supper, they argued, Christ was present at the table holding the bread as he said 'This is my body'. So how could he *literally* mean that the bread was his body? Similarly, now, the body of Christ is ascended and glorified in heaven. So how could he also *physically* be on the altar? Instead

they understood the bread and wine to symbolise the body and blood of Christ – though there was little agreement as to the sense in which they were symbols, as we shall see.

(2) Ridley and the Reformers also maintained that the 'substance' of the bread and wine did not change. 'Substance' is a technical term here. The Catholic church looked back to St Thomas Aquinas (1226-1274) as the 'angelic doctor' who taught the truth about the Eucharist. Aquinas had sought to answer the question, 'If the bread and wine become the body and blood of Christ at the consecration, why do they not change at all in appearance?' His answer had been to distinguish between the *substance* of the bread and wine, their inner essence, their bread-ness and wine-ness, and the *accidents* of the bread and wine, their outward appearance, texture and taste. When the priest recites the words of consecration ('This is my body ... This is my blood'), Aquinas taught, the *substance* of the bread and wine is removed and replaced with the substance of the body and blood of Christ – but the *accidents* remain the same, so that they still go on looking like bread and wine.

Aquinas simply provided a way of explaining what the church had long believed. From as early as the fourth century the view had been widespread that (for instance) 'Before it is consecrated, it is bread; but when the words of Christ are added, it is the body of Christ ... and before the words of Christ,

the cup is full of wine and water; when the words of
Christ have been employed, the blood is created
which redeems his people'. This was written by
Ambrose, Bishop of Milan from 374-397. Other
'Church Fathers' took a different view, rightly
feeling that this explanation undermines the unique
significance of Christ's death on the cross. It makes
him die again at every Eucharist. But this was the
view which prevailed until the Reformation, especially with the support of Aquinas' explanation. It
came to be known as 'transubstantiation', expressing the thought of the change of substance.

Incidentally, the Roman Catholic Church dif-
fered from the Eastern Orthodox Churches just in
what was believed to create the change in the bread
and wine. Was it the recitation of the words of
consecration (the Catholic view), or the prayer for
the Holy Spirit to come down (the Orthodox view)?
Modern liturgies tend to play safe and include both!

(3) The third charge against Ridley was that he
denied that the Mass was a sacrifice, offered for the
living and the dead. This follows from the other
points. For if the substance really does change, as
taught by Aquinas and the church, then the Eucharist becomes a *repetition* or *extension* of Christ's
death, a sacrifice offered by the priest on behalf of
the people. If it does not, then the Eucharist is a
*memorial* of Christ's death, which alone deals with
our sin. Which is it? The Reformers chose the
'memorial' view, although they did not agree over

how we should understand it, as we shall see.

From the earliest years of the church the Eucharist was seen by many as the offering of a sacrifice. It seemed a natural way to think of it. After all, Jesus offered himself as a sacrifice on the cross, and here we are, repeating his action in remembrance of him. The influence of the Old Testament pattern of worship was also a factor: there, a priest offers a sacrifice on behalf of the people, and this was applied to the Eucharist. Why should New Testament worship be less than Old Testament?

Some of the Fathers saw dangers in this way of thinking, and wanted to preserve the uniqueness of Jesus' self-sacrifice on the cross. But generally the language of 'sacrifice' was applied without much hesitation to the Eucharist. This is what Ridley and the Reformers resisted. Ridley wrote, 'Christ's blessed body and blood, which was once only offered and shed upon the cross, being effective for the sins of the whole world, is offered up no more, in the natural substance thereof, neither by the priest, nor any other thing'.

What are we to make of all this today? The views around in the 16th century at the time of the Reformation are all available still, and it will be useful to set out the options, as preparation for looking afresh at the Scriptures. Basically, these views all fall into four groups, with variations within them. We can group them by asking the question, 'How does the Eucharist do good to us, when we partake?' There are basically four answers to that question.

(1) First we must list views we can call *realist*. 'Realist' views are those which say that *the Eucharist does us good because of what we eat*. The bread and wine become in themselves something which nourishes us spiritually, and therefore we are blessed. Of course 'transubstantiation' fits in here, but so also – remarkably! – does the view of Martin Luther, the great German Reformer. Though he objected strongly to the abuses of the Mass, his own thinking about the Eucharist did not differ greatly from the Roman Catholic Church.

Luther's view came to be known as 'consubstantiation'. He himself explained it with the picture of an iron poker pushed into a fire of hot coals. Gradually the poker gets hot and begins to glow, taking on the 'substance' of the fire which is its heat. Just like this, the bread and wine in the Eucharist begin to glow with the presence of Christ, and take on his substance so that when we partake, we are feeding on him.

The word 'transubstantiation' has dropped out of use in the Roman Catholic Church today. Many Catholic writers recognise that there are great difficulties in the way of accepting Aquinas' distinction between substance and accidents as previous generations did. He believed that all objects, not just bread and wine, have an inner substance or essence which is the real 'thing', distinguishable from its particular appearance or make-up. But this simply will not fit with modern physics! So if we want to say that something like this happens to the bread and wine, then we will just have to accept it by faith as something inexplicable.

Many do accept it, of course. But the favoured word amongst Catholic writers at the moment is 'transignification'. This is meant to express the idea that, not the *substance*, but the *significance* of the bread and wine change for us. I have a sick friend, whom I wish to visit. I pick some flowers from the garden to take to her. When I give them, they take on an extra significance as a gift, expressing my love and concern for her. Similarly the bread and wine become significant because they are from God, expressing his love for us in a direct way. To receive them, therefore, is vital to our relationship with him. We will think about this view later: it does not fit well with the other 'realist' views, but may be close to the biblical teaching as we shall see.

(2) Secondly there is the *memorial* view, *which says that the Eucharist does us good because of the way we eat*. Why do we do it at all? Some would reply, *simply because the Lord commanded it* – so that the benefit we get from it is the benefit we always get when we obey his commands, if we eat with a response of faith and love.

This was the view of the Swiss Reformer Ulrich Zwingli. He believed that Christ could not be both in heaven and in the bread and wine on earth – so he rejected the view of his fellow-Reformer Martin Luther, as well as that of the Roman Catholic Church.

He and Luther had a famous debate at Marburg in 1529, but they failed to reach agreement. Luther chalked 'hoc est corpus meum', 'this is my body' on the table between them and simply pointed to it every time Zwingli argued that Jesus could not have meant it literally.

Zwingli's own view was that the bread and wine function simply as a kind of visible parable, picturing Christ's death to us so that we can remember it more effectively, and thus strengthen our faith in him.

This 'memorial' view is the one expressed in the Anglican Book of Common Prayer, which for four centuries formed the basic spiritual diet of millions of Christians worldwide. There the prayer of consecration, after thanking God for the unique and unrepeatable death of Christ, goes on '... and did institute, and in his holy Gospel command us to continue, a **perpetual memory** of that his precious death, until his coming again. Hear us, O merciful Father ... and grant that we, receiving these thy creatures of bread and wine, according to thy Son our Saviour Jesus Christ's holy institution, **in remembrance of** his death and passion, may be partakers of his most blessed body and blood.' Note the words emphasised: it is as we remember that we are able to partake of his body and blood, and this is done by spiritual communion with him.

But these viewpoints are not watertight. By asking that, through the Eucharist, we may *partake* of Christ's body and blood, the Prayer Book moves away from Zwingli and in the direction of the third viewpoint.

(3) Thirdly we may point to views we may loosely call *sacramental* or *symbolic*, which tell us that *the Eucharist does us good because we eat the bread and wine as if we were eating the very flesh of Christ*. The word 'sacrament' is vital here. In spite of his opposition to transubstantiation, our friend Nicholas Ridley could write, 'the bread indeed sacramentally is changed into the body of Christ'. He did not mean that the bread changed in its *material*: the change concerned its 'use, office and dignity'.

What did he mean? He strongly opposed those who (like Zwingli) 'make the holy Sacrament of the blessed body and blood of Christ nothing else, but a bare sign or a figure, to represent Christ none other wise, than the Ivy bush doth represent the wine in a tavern'. (He is thinking of a pub-sign.) It is difficult to pin down exactly what he means by 'sacrament'. The vital thought seems to be: Christ ordained it, with the words 'This is my body ... do this in remembrance of me', and because of that we can be sure that, if we receive it with faith, thankfulness and obedience, we will feed upon Christ himself.

We find the same view in the Westminster

Confession of Faith, the basic statement of faith for all Presbyterian churches worldwide. This teaches that the bread and wine may 'truly, yet sacramentally only' be called the body and blood of Christ (29:5), and that because it is a 'sacrament', we may 'receive and feed upon Christ crucified, and all benefits of his death' when we partake with faith (29:7).

I must confess that I want to know more exactly what is meant by 'sacrament' here. What exactly happens to the bread and the wine, so that they may rightly be called 'the body and blood of Christ'? Do *we* do something to them – setting them apart for use in obedience to Christ's command? Or does *God* do something to them – making them a vehicle of his love and forgiveness? The Reformers tended not to give precise answers to this. The great Swiss Reformer John Calvin emphasised the nature of the Eucharist as 'sacrament', but in explanation of it he wrote (for instance), 'By means of the gospel, and more clearly by the sacred Supper ... Christ offers himself to us with all his blessings, and we receive him in faith'. But what does 'more clearly' mean? Calvin did not believe the same as Zwingli, that the bread and the wine are just a visible picture of something invisible (like the sign outside the pub that pictures the wine inside). But what exactly is added, when we call them 'sacraments'?

Before we turn to the Scriptures, there is one more view to survey:

(4) Fourthly there are views with a *corporate emphasis*, which say that *the Eucharist does us good because of the company with whom we eat*. We may point first (and chiefly) to J. N. Darby and the Brethren as examples here: they emphasised the double meaning of the expression 'body of Christ', which refers both to Christ's own body, represented symbolically by bread and wine, and to the company of believers gathered now in his name, which is also his 'body'. Certainly the apostle Paul uses the term in both senses when he writes about the Eucharist in 1 Corinthians 11, as we shall see. The Brethren saw (and see) the Lord's Supper as the solemn coming-together of God's true people, who recognise and accept each other as the body of Christ when they eat and drink together in fellowship with one another and with him. It means two-directional fellowship, with Christ and with each other – both directions equally important.

This view is growing in strength. One of the criticisms recently thrown at Aquinas by Catholic writers, for instance, has been precisely that he completely ignored the worship-setting for which the bread and wine were being consecrated. The priest might have been doing it alone in a shed on a mountain-top, for all the difference it made to Aquinas' understanding of what was happening. This cannot be right! The context of it, the worshipping congregation and the fellowship of the wider church, must surely be vital.

Similarly the second and third viewpoints both tend to be individualistic: the whole transaction takes place just between me and the Lord. I could be on my own in a field, for all the difference made by those around me.

However, there were nods in the direction of this 'corporate' view in the Westminster Confession of Faith, and in the 39 Articles of the Church of England. The Westminster Confession, while basically taking a 'sacramental' view (see above), also says that the Lord's Supper is 'a bond and pledge of (our) communion with him, and with each other, as members of his mystical body' (29:1). And Article 28 of the 39 Articles, 'Of the Lord's Supper', begins, 'The Supper of the Lord is not only a sign of the love that Christians ought to have among themselves one to another ...'. This fits with the Reformers' practice: Nicholas Ridley, for instance, on becoming Bishop of Rochester in 1547, immediately banned solitary Masses in his diocese. Communion could only be celebrated within a company of God's people.

The lesser-known English Reformer John Frith, who was martyred in 1533, strongly emphasised this aspect of the Eucharist. So also did some of the early Baptists at this time. On the basis of Paul's teaching in 1 Corinthians 11, some of them even thought that believers must regard all their possessions as belonging to the 'body' as a whole.

These four views are not mutually exclusive. In

particular (2), (3) and (4) can be combined in various ways. But the absolutely crucial thing in all this is *not to be bound by any human or ecclesiastical tradition, but to be ready to think afresh on the basis of the Scriptures*. And I believe that, when we do this, these questions and issues lose their puzzles and things start to come clear. That is what we will now do!

# Part Two:
# Back to Basics

Our minds are full of questions as we turn to the Bible. What does it teach about the Eucharist? In particular:

* What guidance does it give about 'doing' it properly? May anyone 'do' it, at any time, or must there be a priest or church minister in charge? How often should we take communion? Does it matter?

* In what kind of spiritual state should we be, in order to receive communion? Should we hold back from taking it if we are feeling particularly sinful and out of fellowship with God? – or if we have had a row at home beforehand?

* Does the Bible give answers to any of the questions which have so long troubled the church, and which people still ask: what *does* happen to the bread and the wine? Do they change in some way? How do they become a means of blessing for us? In what sense do they 'become' the body and blood of Christ?

All these issues will gradually be tackled, as we look at the biblical teaching. We will do it in three stages. First we will look at the Last Supper, at which Jesus instituted the Eucharist. What exactly did he do? How did the disciples understand his strange actions? What exactly was he telling them

– and us – to do, when he said, 'Do this in remembrance of me'?

Secondly, we will look at Paul's teaching in 1 Corinthians, where most of two chapters (10-11) is devoted to the topic. What problem was Paul facing, and what was his response? Why does he say what he says? He has some big surprises in store.

Then thirdly, we will tackle an unusual topic, but one which I believe is very helpful as biblical background for our understanding of the Eucharist: we will think about *prophetic signs* in the Bible and discover something vital, not only about the Eucharist, but also (I believe) about baptism.

So that's our agenda for Part Two of this book!

# 7. What did Jesus do at the Last Supper?

We have five accounts of the Last Supper – one in each of the Gospels, and one in 1 Corinthians 11:23-26. Interestingly the institution of the Lord's Supper, as something to be celebrated by the church, is only described in two of these accounts, those of Luke and of Paul. Only they record the command of Jesus: 'Do this in remembrance of me'.

Matthew and Mark simply describe – in almost identical words – Jesus' actions in taking, giving thanks for, breaking and distributing the bread with the words 'take, eat, this is my body' (Matt. 26:26; Mark 14:22), and then taking, giving thanks for and handing round the cup, with the words 'this is my blood of the covenant, which is shed for many [*Matthew adds:*] for the forgiveness of sins' (Matt. 26:27f.; Mark 14:23f). Then they both record Jesus' comment, 'I tell you, I will not drink again of the fruit of the vine until that day, when I drink it new with you in the kingdom of my Father', and mention that they all then sang a hymn and went out to the Mount of Olives (Matt. 26:29f.; Mark 14:25f.).

So, strictly speaking, Matthew's and Mark's

readers would not have gathered that they should try to re-create the Last Supper in any sense. Of course, this does not mean that Matthew and Mark were opposed to doing this. In all likelihood, both they and their readers took it for granted.

The same is probably the case with John. In his description of the Last Supper (John 13:1-30), he strangely omits all mention of Jesus' symbolic actions with the bread and the wine. Instead, he focuses on the moment during the meal when Jesus rose from the table, girded himself with a towel, and washed his disciples' feet.

None of the other Gospels record this incident. Some experts have concluded that John wanted to downplay the place of the Eucharist in the life of the church. He does not mention it, they say, because he was against it. But again, this is unlikely. As is often the case, it is more likely that John is deliberately supplementing what his readers already know. They were expecting to read about the institution of the Lord's Supper. Instead, they hear Jesus' teaching about mutual service and self-giving (see especially John 13:12-17).

This is exactly the teaching that both Paul and Luke give in connection with the Eucharist! Paul rebukes the Corinthians for their divisions and lack of mutual care when they gather, which mean altogether that 'it is not the Lord's Supper which you eat' (1 Cor. 11:20). And Luke follows his account of the institution with the horrible story of how a 'dispute broke out among them (the disciples), as to which of them was the greatest' (Luke 22:24). So human! Jesus' response is beautiful, and all the more poignant if he had just washed their feet, or was doing it even as he spoke:

> 'The kings of the nations lord it over their subjects, and the powerful like to be called "benefactors". But you must be different. Let the great among you be like the youngest, and let the leader be like the servant. For who is greater, the one who reclines at table, or the one who serves? Is it not the one who reclines at table? But I am among you as one who serves!' (Luke 22:25-27).

Some churches, for instance the Mennonites, practise mutual feet-washing at Communion, in direct imitation of Jesus' action and to express this commitment to each other.

Both Luke and John seem to be concerned about status-seeking in the church, and particularly in connection with the Eucharist. It must not be the means of personal exaltation at the expense of fellow-believers. If only the church had heeded this prophetic warning! It did not take long for church leadership to become a matter of status, rather than servant-hood, particularly when the power to lead the celebration of the Eucharist was restricted to the priesthood.

So what happened at the Last Supper? Already we can see that some unusual things occurred. None of the disciples expected to have their feet washed by their 'Teacher and Lord' (John 13:13). In fact, this was only one of several strange things which happened that night and which must have left the disciples feeling puzzled, afraid and excited all at once. In order to pick out the things that would have stood out for them, we need to take a step back and ask what they expected as they came together for that Passover meal.

Passover was probably the second 'biggest' Jewish festival, second only to Tabernacles which in the time of Jesus drew the largest crowds to Jerusalem. But even if Tabernacles was bigger, Jesus and his disciples were probably sharing Jerusalem with about 100,000 other visitors that night. No wonder Jesus had to make arrangements in advance for the room (Matt. 26:18f.; Mark 14:12-16; Luke 22:7-13). It was the festival at which Israel remembered and celebrated the Exodus from Egypt. The Jewish Mishnah, although written some 200 years after the time of Jesus, is very helpful in conveying the feeling of Passover:

> In every generation a man must so regard himself as if he came forth himself out of Egypt, for it is written, 'And thou shalt tell thy son in that day saying, It is because of that which the Lord did for me when I came forth out of Egypt'.

Therefore are we bound to give thanks, to praise, to glorify, to honour, to exalt, to extol and to bless him who wrought all these wonders for our fathers and for us. He brought us out from bondage to freedom, from sorrow to gladness, and from mourning to a Festival-day, and from darkness to great light, and from servitude to redemption; so let us say before him the Hallelujah!

This *Hallelujah!* is a reference to the so-called 'Hallel' or 'Praise' Psalms which were especially appointed for Passover: Psalms 113-118. The 'hymn' sung by Jesus and his disciples as they left for the Garden of Gethsemane will have been the second group of these Psalms, probably 115-118. That, at least, happened according to the usual pattern! (Incidentally, it is worth noticing how suitable these Psalms are for what Jesus is about to experience – especially Psalms 116 and 118.)

This passage from the Mishnah shows how Passover worked. Each Israelite had to identify himself or herself with the Exodus generation, with those who actually left Egypt. It was not just a matter of commemorating an important event. People had to celebrate the event *as if they themselves had taken part in it*. And this was not difficult. For the event in question had actually created what they now were, God's people living in the land to which he had brought them from Egypt. Through the annual Passover celebration, each Israelite reaffirmed his or her personal participation in the great events which shaped Israel's identity.

Sacrificing a lamb, just as the Exodus generation had done, helped in this identification. Just as they had sheltered under the blood of a sacrifice (Exodus 12:13), so now each family or group had to sacrifice a lamb in the Temple (while it still stood), and depend on its blood for salvation. They would eat the meat at the Passover meal, just as Israel did on the night before the Exodus.

This helps us to understand the Eucharist. Jesus' command, 'Do this in remembrance of *me*' should be translated like this, with emphasis on 'me'. In other words, there is an implied negative in the command, which the disciples would certainly have grasped: Jesus was telling them to celebrate the Passover *no longer* in remembrance of the Exodus, *but instead* in remembrance of himself. This had profound implications for the disciples. It touched their whole identity. Are they Jews, remembering with thankfulness God's deliverance of their nation from slavery into freedom? No more. Their identity as disciples of Jesus Christ now takes over.

And the new foundational event to which remembrance is directed? ... well, it must have been only later that the disciples realised the significance of the action which preceded Jesus' words, the breaking and distributing of the unleavened bread with the comment 'This is my body which is

given for you'. His death takes over from the
Exodus as the foundational event, but the style of
remembering remains the same. We celebrate his
death with that same sense that this is the event
which shapes our whole identity and gives meaning
to our existence. It is an event in which we, his
people, participate together.

Let us think further about the bread. In the
Passover meal, the unleavened bread was usually
eaten just before the main course, after the second
cup of wine. Luke refers to this second cup in his
account (Luke 22:17f) – in fact, he attaches to this
cup Jesus' saying about not drinking wine again,
this side of the Kingdom. Normally, the head of the
house would then give thanks over the unleavened
bread, and this would be eaten just before the main
course – the Passover lamb – was served.

None of the accounts of the Last Supper mention
a lamb. We cannot say for sure that there was no
lamb at that Passover meal, but it looks unlikely
that there was – not just because no lamb is mentioned, but also because it seems that *another of the
strange things about that meal was that it happened
a day early*. John helps us here.

The other three Gospels all clearly identify the
Last Supper as a Passover meal, but Matthew drops
a hint which John develops and clarifies. In Matthew, Jesus' disciples ask him 'on the first day of
the Passover' where he would like them to prepare
the meal (Matt. 26:17). This would have been the

thirteenth day of the month Nisan, the day on which
all leaven (yeast) and bread made with yeast had to
be removed from people's homes. Normally, the
Passover meal was eaten on the fifteenth day of
Nisan, and the Festival lasted until the twenty-first.

Jesus sends his disciples to prepare the meal
with the words, 'Go into the city to ... and say to
him, "The teacher says, 'My time has come and I
want to celebrate Passover with my disciples at
your home' " ' (Matt. 26:18). The disciples obey,
and then we read, 'When evening came, Jesus
reclined at table with his disciples ...' (Matt. 26:20).
The implication seems to be that they ate on the
evening of that same day – which would have been
reckoned as the beginning of Nisan 14, since days
ran from evening to evening. 'My time has come'
is, of course, looking forward to the crucifixion, but
addressed to the landlord of the Passover-room, it
sounds like a request to celebrate Passover at 'my
time'.

John makes this crystal clear. He leaves us in no
doubt that the Last Supper took place on the day
*before* Passover. Not only does he begin his
account of it with the comment that it took place
'before the feast of the Passover' (John 13:1), but
he also goes out of his way to tell us that the next
morning Jesus' accusers did not want to enter
Pilate's residence 'so that they might not be de-
filed, but might be able to eat the Passover'. It had
not yet taken place.

The reason for John's emphasis appears later. He tells us (19:14) that Jesus was condemned to die at the sixth hour (i.e. about midday) on the day of *preparation for* the Passover (i.e. Nisan 14), and that he died during the course of that afternoon. The Jews took quick action to make sure that none of the bodies remained on the crosses after dusk and into Nisan 15, the Passover day, which was also a Sabbath that year (19:31).

All Jewish readers, familiar with the festival, would have known what John was saying: *Jesus died at exactly the time when the Passover lambs were being sacrificed in the Temple*, in preparation for the meals to take place all over the city that evening. John rubs his point home by quoting Exodus 12:46: 'These things took place so that the Scripture might be fulfilled, "Not a single bone of it shall be broken"' (John 19:36): this is actually an instruction about the treatment of the Passover lamb!

It is very unlikely that Jesus and his disciples would have been able to acquire a lamb a day early for their own meal. We cannot be certain of this, of course, but I believe we will rightly catch the significance of what happened at their meal if we imagine it taking place without a lamb.

Here is the scene: the disciples are puzzled as to why the meal is taking place a day early. They have no lamb as a result. They reach the point of the meal where the lamb would be normally eaten, following the unleavened bread. Jesus takes the bread, gives thanks, breaks and distributes it, saying, 'This is my body, which is given for you'. Is there an implied negative there, too? 'Not the Passover lamb, but my body is given for you ...'. The absence of a lamb is no obstacle. Far from it. In fact, the Lamb is not absent at all, as John realised later. Jesus is 'the Lamb of God, who takes away the sin of the world' (John 1:29), the one who is the 'bread from heaven' who gives his flesh for the life of the world (John 6:51), and who died at the moment the lambs were being sacrificed.

'This is my body', therefore, *must* have symbolic force, because the body of Jesus, given for us, is his physical body which hung and died upon the cross the following afternoon. Jesus anticipates that event by re-writing the Passover liturgy and turning the bread into a symbol of his own death – in the absence of a Passover lamb.

The same thing happens with the cup. After the meal, the Passover would normally continue with the third cup, known as 'the cup of blessing', again accompanied by a thanksgiving. Jesus performs the thanksgiving all right, but then again re-writes the liturgy (a) by not drinking it himself, and (b) by attaching a completely new significance to it. We must think about each of these strange departures from normal practice.

First, Jesus' new words. The wording of the four accounts differ, but all agree (a) that Jesus made the wine a symbol of his blood, and (b) that he spoke of the covenant. 'This is my blood of the covenant which is poured out for many' (Mark, the shortest); 'This cup is the new covenant in my blood. Do this, as often as you drink it, in remembrance of me' (Paul, the longest). Once again, the thought of replacement is clear. *Not* the blood of the Passover lamb, but *my* blood must be remembered. Paul and Luke both refer to the new covenant, and this simply strengthens the thought that the old is being set aside, and God is doing something new.

Jeremiah had prophesied a 'new covenant', which would finally deal with the intractable sin of Israel (Jer. 31:31-34). Previously, the old covenant had been sealed and ratified by blood: 'Moses then took the blood, sprinkled it on the people, and said, "This is the blood of the covenant that the LORD has made with you" ' (Exod. 24:8). Jeremiah does not mention the blood which will ratify and seal the new covenant – but Jesus does. It is to be his own blood, that is, his life. By using the very words of Moses from Exodus 24:8, Jesus again introduces the thought of replacement: not by the blood of a sacrificial animal, but through his own death, God brings Israel into relationship with himself and makes them his own (that is the meaning of 'covenant') – and not just Israel, but 'many' (shorthand for 'the whole world').

Secondly, we note Jesus' remarkable abstention from this 'cup of blessing' – and also from the fourth cup of wine with which the meal usually ended. In fact, it seems as if none of them drank the final cup that night. According to Luke, Jesus distributed the second cup and then announced that he would not drink again of the fruit of the vine until the Kingdom comes (Luke 22:17f.). So when he blesses the third cup, he does not drink, but passes it to the disciples, describing it as 'my blood, which is shed for many'.

Describing it in this way, it would actually be inappropriate for him to drink it himself. And that unlocks another unusual feature of the meal that night: normally, each person would have their own cup at the table, and it would be the task of the host to fill the cups and to give thanks, before each person – including the host – drank individually. But Jesus passes his own cup around the table, and 'they all drank from it' (Mark 14:23). It becomes a direct and personal gift from him, which they receive. Whereas the 'cup of blessing' was meant just to express Israel's praise and gratitude for the Exodus, now it takes on a much deeper significance.

The 'cup' remaining for Jesus is the one he faces later that evening in the Garden of Gethsemane. He prays that, if possible, the cup might pass from him (Mark 14:36). But he knows that, unless he drinks it, he could not offer that other cup to his disciples, the one that represents his blood shed for them.

There is some evidence that, already, Jews

thought of the Passover meal as a foretaste or anticipation of the 'Messianic banquet', the great meal at which finally the Messiah would be host to his people in his Kingdom. The fourth and final cup – which none of them drank, it seems – was known as the 'cup of consummation', looking forward to that Kingdom feast. Jesus tells his disciples that this is his last Passover meal until the Kingdom comes. As we shall see in the next chapter, Paul picks up this thought when he describes the Eucharist as 'proclaiming the death of the Lord until he comes' (1 Cor. 11:26).

But the disciples must go on drinking the third cup, the 'cup of blessing': 'Do this in remembrance of me'. In explaining this command, some have suggested that we are not so much to remind *ourselves* of Jesus through our continued celebration; rather, we are to remind *God* of Jesus – bringing to *God's* 'remembrance' what he has done in Christ, and therefore (implicitly) asking him to continue to be gracious to us because of Jesus. On this ground, some have defended a sacrificial understanding of the Eucharist: we offer Christ up to God for his remembrance. Could this be right?

In response, we must say that this explanation moves far beyond the original Passover context of Jesus' words. The point of the Passover was not to remind God of what he had done, but to reinforce the memory of it among the beneficiaries of the Exodus, and to allow them joyfully to celebrate their membership of the people formed by that event. This must be the sense in which Jesus used the word 'remembrance', focusing it now upon himself.

Of course, each year families had to sacrifice a lamb, so Passover had a strongly sacrificial element within it. But it would be wrong to apply this to the Eucharist (even though these Old Testament ideas of sacrifice and priesthood were very quickly applied to the Eucharist in the early church). At the Last Supper Jesus deliberately set aside the use of a sacrificial lamb, and focused all the 'remembering' onto himself and the shedding of his own blood.

What is the 'this', which Jesus tells his disciples to 'do'? It is really shorthand for 'celebrate the Passover'. In Matthew 26:18 Jesus uses the same word when he tells the landlord, 'I want to "do" the Passover with my disciples at your house'. It does not just refer to repeating Jesus' actions with the bread and wine. Jesus is telling his disciples – us – that we, his church, must maintain a celebration like the Passover meal, but focusing now on his death rather than on the Exodus.

That is just how Paul thinks of the Eucharist. 'Clear away the old yeast, so that you may be true to your nature as unleavened bread!', he tells the Corinthians, using the picture of that annual clear-out on Nisan 13. 'For our Passover lamb has been sacrificed – Christ. So let us celebrate the feast, not with the old yeast of evil and wickedness, but with the unleavened bread of sincerity and truth' (1 Cor. 5:7f). Later in the same letter he develops this teaching about the Eucharist, and specifically calls the cup 'the cup of blessing' (1 Cor. 10:16).

Finally, let us ask how the disciples would have reacted to the fact that Jesus made these surprising alterations to the Passover. Strangely, though they must have been surprised by what he did, I do not think they would have been surprised that he did this kind of thing. They were used to him doing and saying the most unexpected things. They had just watched him commandeer someone's donkey to ride into Jerusalem, curse a fig tree, throw money-changers out of the Temple, denounce the scribes and Pharisees very powerfully, and predict the total destruction of the Temple. And that was just in the last three days! His whole ministry had been full of such things – not least the frequent occasions on which, with a word of command, he had healed the sick and demon-possessed.

We do not know what the disciples thought about Jesus at this point. But one explanation lay close at hand, and this was used by many people, including the disciples: *these are the actions of a prophet*. It is typical of prophets that they speak words and perform actions from God that surprise, shock, and speak with power. The disciples would have understood Jesus' actions and words at the Last Supper as *prophetic*. This point is so important for our understanding of the Eucharist that we will devote a whole chapter to it (chapter 9).

Let us now summarise what we have discovered, and draw some conclusions. The Last Supper was a most remarkable meal, in several respects:

\* It took place a day early, and probably no lamb was eaten. Thus it was distanced to some extent from the general Passover celebrations – and this suited Jesus' purpose. He wanted to rebuild Passover around himself.

\* Jesus added words to the Passover liturgy, turning the unleavened bread and the cup of blessing into symbols of his impending death – thus making the Passover into a memorial of himself, rather than of the Exodus.

\* A single cup was used, rather than individual cups, and (probably feeling rather puzzled) the disciples all drank from it as Jesus said, 'This is my blood of the covenant'.

\* In his words Jesus not only applied the Passover to himself, but also claimed to be the fulfilment of Jeremiah 31:31-34, the prophecy of the new covenant.

\* He also invited the disciples to look ahead with him, from this meal to the Messianic banquet in the

Kingdom. Before then, *we* will drink, but *he* will not.

* Finally the whole meal was truncated. Jesus did not drink the third cup, and the fourth was probably abandoned altogether. Instead of spending the night in quiet prayer (the usual practice), the whole company got up and went out to the Garden of Gethsemane, where the drama of the Passion began to unfold.

What conclusions should we draw? We must listen particularly carefully to our Lord Jesus himself. We must not find ourselves doing in his name things which he did not intend!

(1) The Eucharist is a memorial feast like the Passover. But unlike the Passover, it does not involve a sacrifice. Jesus dispensed with the lamb, because it is no longer needed. We remember his death for us as the totally sufficient ground of our salvation.

(2) The Eucharist is a community *event*. It celebrates our common identity as the people of God, constituted by the death of Christ. Solitary celebration, and solitary participation, are both alike inappropriate. We need to make sure that our Eucharists express this 'together' quality.

(3) The Eucharist is a community *action*. It is something which all the disciples are to 'do'. Just as the Passover was celebrated by each family group,

or group of friends or disciples, so the Eucharist is an action performed by each Christian family group, i.e. each local church. It is not an action performed by a minister and observed or joined by the congregation. If a minister leads, he or she does so embodying the action which is properly the congregation's. We do it, together. The minister stands at the communion table representing not Christ, but the congregation – just as the head of each house represented his family as he led the Passover liturgy.

(4) Since Jesus was clearly employing the bread and the cup as symbols of himself, we should do the same. The unleavened bread was already a symbol of the Exodus, reminding the Israelites of their hasty departure from Egypt. Jesus diverts the symbol to himself. Any literal interpretation of 'this is my body', therefore, will be inappropriate.

(5) The Eucharist looks in two directions simultaneously: back to the cross, and forward to the Kingdom. We drink from a cup which is a *tiny foretaste* of the 'cup of consummation' awaiting us at the Lord's table in glory!

(6) Finally, it is appropriate if we think of this Last Supper/Passover as providing the *pattern* for the way we should celebrate the Eucharist. Dom Gregory Dix, whose book I mentioned right at the start in chapter one, is famous for his emphasis on the 'fourfold action' of Christ as the pattern for the Eucharist. Virtually all modern Communion litur-

gies have followed Dix' recommendation in his book, which was significantly called *The Shape of the Liturgy*. He pointed out that Jesus (1) took, (2) blessed, (3) broke, and (4) gave the bread, and then repeated three of these actions for the wine (took, blessed, gave). Following this pattern, many modern services draw distinct attention to each of these actions.

It would be possible to overemphasise this in a semi-magical way, as though it could not be a 'proper' Eucharist unless each action were performed. If these actions help to remind us of the original Passover setting, then they perform a useful function.

There is more yet to be discovered from these passages, particularly when we explore the nature of 'prophetic signs' in chapter 9. But now we should turn to Paul.

# 8. Problems and answers in Corinth

Paul's relationship with the church in Corinth was a stormy one. He had spent about two years ministering there (Acts 18:1-18), but problems brewed soon after his departure, in several respects. Already, by the time of writing 1 Corinthians (probably eighteen months to two years later), Paul had had to write to them about their behaviour, and they had chosen to misunderstand what he wrote (1 Cor. 5:9-11). So what we know as his *first* letter to Corinth was in fact at least his second, and was prompted (a) by a letter from them, asking about some of their difficulties (1 Cor. 7:1), and (b) by his own awareness of other problems they had not mentioned (see e.g. 1 Cor. 1:11, 5:1)!

This is relevant for us, because his teaching about the Eucharist in 1 Corinthians 10-11 is prompted by one problem of each type – one they had asked him about, and one they had not. They themselves asked him about the problem of meat offered to idols (see 8:1), and Paul devotes three chapters to dealing with that (chapters 8-10). But he was aware of a further problem about which they were not nearly so concerned as he: their divided-ness.

He mentions right at the start his concern that they have fallen into factions. 'I gather from some of Chloe's household that there are rivalries among you. I am referring to the fact that each of you is proclaiming a loyalty, "I follow Paul", or "I follow Apollos", or "I follow Cephas", or "I follow Christ"' (1:11f.). For Paul this state of internal rivalry was *a fundamental challenge to their whole identity as a church*. 'Is Christ divided?' is his immediate response (1:13) – and that about sums up the essence of his challenge to them. He returns to this theme of the unity of the church throughout the letter, in different ways – most notably in chapters 12-14 where he deals with the issue of spiritual gifts and the nature of the church as the one body of Christ, endowed with a variety of different gifts and ministries by the Spirit. But he also returns to it in his teaching about the Eucharist in chapters 10-11, especially in 11:17-34.

I must say I am firmly of the opinion that Paul would regard our denominational loyalties as nega-tively as he regarded the factions in Corinth. 'I follow Rome', 'I follow Calvin', 'I follow Cupitt', 'I follow Wimber': he would tell us all very directly that we must abandon these human loyalties that keep us apart. The issue of truth is vitally important, of course, and Paul would not compromise on that. But he would tell us, as he told the Corinthians, that the truth is far greater than one person's grasp of it, however great that person may be. There is only one foundation on which we must build, and that is Jesus Christ, and not any lesser person (3:11). To divide the church is to destroy the Temple of God in which his Spirit lives, and that is a terrible thing (3:16f.)!

Sometimes, of course, we have to take a stand for Christian truth against abuse. But, Paul would say: woe betide those who let such occasions divide the church! The treatment handed out to Nicholas Ridley, at the last hearing before his execution, was an absolute disgrace.

Though Ridley was a Bishop, and a man of great learning and piety, Bishop White of Lincoln crudely insulted his views about the Eucharist, and refused to let him read a prepared statement. Then when Ridley asked for permission to speak 'forty words', White counted the words on his fingers and silenced him when he got to forty.

Could they not pray together? Could they not explain their mind to each other in a spirit of openness and brotherhood? Even if ultimately they could not reach agreement, could they not respect the integrity of each other's viewpoint? This kind of rivalry was going on all over 'Christian' Europe in the sixteenth century. May the twentieth – and twenty-first – do better, for Christ's sake.

The church in Corinth was divided not just by religious factions, but also by social make-up. It is true that among them there were 'not many wise in human terms, not many powerful, not many of noble birth' (1:26), but there were certainly a few in those categories – perhaps a sizeable minority. Going to law was a costly activity, and Paul rebukes Christians for taking each other to court in 6:1-6. As we shall see, it was particularly these economic divisions that were manifesting themselves at the Lord's Supper.

We start with the problem they present to Paul, that of eating meat offered to idols. The problem is quite simply explained.

Corinth had very many pagan temples, dedicated to a vast number of different deities, and animal sacrifice was constantly carried out in them all. In fact, most of the meat on sale in the marketplace would actually have been slaughtered in one of the temples, 'officially' as a sacrifice to the god.

In addition, many of the temples had trade-guilds associated with them (silversmiths, weavers, olive-growers, potters), and these guilds would often hold festivals which would involve worship in the temple followed by a feast in one of the side-rooms provided for the purpose. Private individuals might hire these rooms also, for celebrations of any kind.

The question was: what should Christians do about both these facts of life in Corinth? (1) Should they buy meat in the marketplace? And (2), more pressingly, if their own trade-guild held a festival, or if they were invited to a private celebration in a temple, should they participate? Non-participation could have serious social and economic consequences. They might forfeit their membership of their trade-guild. They certainly could not aspire to leadership of it without participating in these pagan celebrations.

They did not ask Paul about the Lord's Supper. He brings that topic up, in answer to these two issues, particularly the second. What does he say?

First, he accepts the argument of the 'don't ask questions – just eat up' lobby. Yes, he says, 'we know that an idol is nothing really, and there is no God but one' (8:4). In theory, therefore, it is permissible to disregard the origin of the meat as a pagan sacrifice, and just accept it gratefully (whether bought or given), because 'for us there is one God, the Father from whom all things come and to whom we belong, and one Lord, Jesus Christ, through whom all things come and through whom we exist' (8:6).

But this liberty must be voluntarily curbed if it creates a stumbling-block for someone who just cannot escape the feeling that eating such meat means worshipping the idol to which it was offered (8:7). Paul calls such a person 'weak', but the weak need to be cared for. The point is not that the opinions of such a 'weak' person would be offended by seeing a fellow-Christian eating idol-meat in a pagan temple, but that *he might be led to do it himself* – and for him this would be defilement and would lead to his destruction (8:10f.). Your freedom, says Paul, must not produce the destruction of someone for whom Christ died.

Paul really underlines this point, with a whole chapter devoted to the theme of strenuous self-sacrifice for the good of others (chapter 9). In the way Paul tackles the question they raise, we can discern his interest in the question they do not raise, that of the unity of the church, its mutual care and service.

Why would it destroy a 'weak' person, to eat in a pagan temple? This is where Paul brings in the Lord's Supper. At this point, I think it would be useful to pause in your reading of this book and read 1 Corinthians 10:1-22. Reflect on what Paul writes for a while, before coming back to this page.

Idolatry, Paul says, is death-dealing. Israel fell into idolatry during the wilderness wanderings, and the result was death (10:7-10) – in spite of the fact that the Israelites had enjoyed a close spiritual relationship with God. In 10:1-4 he describes that relationship in Christian terms: they had been baptised (by their immersion in the pillar of cloud and in the Red Sea, 10:2) and were feeding on spiritual food from God, represented by the manna and the miraculous gift of water from the rock (10:3f.). He even says, 'the Rock was Christ' (10:4)! But in spite of these gifts and privileges, they fell into idolatry and were destroyed.

Paul admits that he is treating the story of Israel in the wilderness typologically (10:6,11). That is to say, he is aware that he cannot really regard the Israelites of old as Christians indistinguishable from the Corinthians. But *what happened to them represents in pictorial form the possibilities that face the Corinthians*. They too enjoy a deep relationship with God, symbolised by baptism, and by eating and drinking; and they too could throw it all away by falling into idolatry.

The point is: even if idols are 'nothing', to worship an idol by eating in its temple is to offer sacrifice to demons, rather than to God (10:20). It means bringing yourself into a dangerous spiritual realm of real contact with forces which can destroy you. That was what happened to Israel in the wilderness, and Paul is clearly fearful lest the same should happen to his Corinthians. On the other hand, we too, like Israel, have spiritual food to sustain our relationship with God: 'the cup of blessing which we bless, is it not a fellowship in the blood of Christ? The bread which we break, is it not a fellowship in the body of Christ?' (10:16). The contrast between the two possibilities helps us to clarify his positive understanding of the Eucharist.

Feeding in a pagan temple, for someone whose conscience is 'weak' and who still 'believes' in the existence of pagan gods, even though she does not worship them, will mean a real contact with the spiritual forces of evil which rule there. Conversely drinking the 'cup of blessing' and eating the broken bread will mean, for a Christian believer, a real 'fellowship' with the body and blood of Christ. 'I do not want you to have fellowship with demons!' he warns them. 'You cannot drink the cup of the Lord and the cup of demons; you cannot partake at the table of the Lord and at the table of demons' (10:20f.).

This is most important. I believe that Paul would be disappointed by the views of Ulrich Zwingli (details above in Part One!). Paul treats the bread and wine of the Eucharist here in serious terms. To eat them is to 'participate' in the body and blood of Christ. He does not define precisely how this occurs. The contrast with idolatry helps us to understand a little – to participate in idolatry means coming under the malign influence of demonic powers, and in the same way to participate in the table of the Lord means creating spiritual communion ('fellowship') with him. We can say more about how it works, I believe, but that must wait for the next chapter.

The word 'fellowship' is important here (the famous Greek word *koinonia*). Paul uses it with a double significance. It indicates the spiritual contact, the *vertical interaction*, between the worshipper and either the demons or Christ. It also indicates the human bonding, the *horizontal interaction* between the body of fellow-worshippers. This comes out particularly in 10:17. In the preceding verses

Paul has focused on the vertical kind of fellowship, the spiritual engagement with Christ (or demons). Then following 10:16, quoted above ('the bread which we break, is it not a fellowship in the body of Christ?'), he goes on, 'for we, being many, are one bread and one body, for we all partake of the one bread' (10:17).

This makes it clear that he is also thinking of horizontal *koinonia* between believers. The eating and drinking which is Christian worship means two-directional fellowship, with Christ himself (fellowship *in* his body) and with the others at the table (fellowship *with* his body). And the vertical cements the horizontal: we are one body *for* we all partake of the one bread.

This is most important. At the end of the chapter we will reflect on some of the implications of this for our worship today. But first we must look on to the second part of Paul's eucharistic teaching, in 11:17-34.

As Paul moves forward in his letter, the issue of the unity of the church (never far from his mind) becomes more prominent. In 11:2-16 he touches on the unity of man and woman in the ministry of the church – an area where he feels the Corinthians are doing quite well (11:2). But then he turns to an area where they are definitely not doing well, he says (11:17) – their celebrations of the Lord's Supper. And in a nutshell, the problem with their celebra-tions is that they have become occasions for reinforcing *dis*unity, rather than expressing and deepening their *koinonia* with each other.

11:17-22 makes this crystal clear. There are divisions among them when they come together. 'For when you eat, each of you just goes ahead with his own meal, so that one person is hungry while another is drunk. Do you not have homes in which to eat and drink? Or do you want to despise the church of God, and to put the poor to shame?' (11:21f.). This is obviously directed at the wealthier members of the church, and at their lack of care for the poorer ones. The wealthy, instead of providing carefully for the poor, were simply neglecting them and using the Lord's Supper as an opportunity for self-indulgence. In Corinth at this time, it appears that the Lord's Supper was a full church meal – except that it was not. Because of these divisions and lack of care, 'when you come together it is *not* the Lord's Supper that you eat!' (11:20).

This is remarkable. The Mediaeval church conducted long discussions about what constituted a valid or invalid Eucharist. If an adulterer or unbeliever eats consecrated bread, does he eat the body of Christ? If a mouse creeps in and consumes the reserved sacrament, does it eat the body of Christ? If the priest is a fornicator or murderer, is his consecration valid? Can a priest consecrate bread and wine at a distance? Could he turn all the bread in a marketplace into the body of Christ at once? Generally speaking, the view prevailed that, since it was the words that made the change ('this is my body ... this is my blood'), it did not matter what was the spiritual state of the consecrating priest or the identity of the receiver. Yes, said Aquinas, the mouse does eat the body of Christ. But he drew the line before some of these absurdities: he taught that consecration could only take place in the presence of the priest, and in quantities appropriate for a church-full of people.

If only they had listened to Paul! He says quite explicitly that *a Eucharist conducted in a divided church, a church out of love with itself, is invalid.* 'It is not the Lord's Supper that you eat'. That is the only case he seems to envisage. There can be no *koinonia* with the Lord, if there is no *koinonia* between his people. All the other questions, about who presides and what words are said, seem quite beside the point. When Paul records the words of Jesus in (11:24f.), his purpose is not to make sure that they are using the right formula in consecrating the bread and wine. He does so in order to remind them who and what they are remembering: they are remembering the total self-giving of Christ, represented vividly in the broken bread and wine. How can they do this, while neglecting and spurning the needs of others around them? In fact, the Lord's Supper *cannot* be celebrated under such circumstances. This is both clear, and very challenging.

But their celebrations were not just invalid. Further, Paul saw grave *dangers* for the Corinthian

church in holding Eucharists under these circumstances. 'He who eats and drinks without discerning the body eats and drinks judgment upon himself!' (11:29). Already, he says, because of their
abuses, some of them have died, and many of them
are sick (11:30) – a judgment from God which was
meant to correct them and deliver them from final
condemnation (11:32). We have completely lost
this perspective on our Eucharists today, it seems to
me. Where is the sense that we are dicing with death
if we abuse them, treat them lightly, engage in them
while out of love with others in the fellowship?

Of course, it would be possible to overplay this
'warning' element. The Eucharist is meant to be a
glad celebration, like Passover – Paul would be the
first to agree with this. We must not make it fearful
or forbidding. But we must take seriously what Paul
says here. He does not mince his words. He tells us
straight that 'whoever eats the bread and drinks the
cup of the Lord unworthily, will be guilty of the
body and blood of the Lord' (11:27). What does
'unworthily' mean here? Not surprisingly, some
Christians have abstained from Communion for
many years, for fear of not taking it 'worthily' and
falling under this guilt. What exactly is the abuse Paul
is attacking?

The phrase 'without discerning the body' in
11:29 sums it up. This has a double meaning, in line
with the double meaning of 'body' in (10:16f.), and
the vertical and horizontal dimensions of *koinonia*.

It means, first, 'without discerning the body and blood of Christ in the bread and wine'. The abuse is to partake lightly or flippantly, without taking seriously the fellowship with Christ which eating means.

Then secondly it means 'without discerning his body in those around us', that is, without realising that 'his body' is represented before us, not just in the bread and wine, but also in all our brothers and sisters for whom he died. Paul will move on, in the next chapter, to explore in detail what it means that the church is 'the body of Christ' into which we have all been baptised by one Spirit (12:12f.).

These two meanings are inseparable. We cannot 'discern the body' in one sense, while failing to discern it in the other sense. To be 'guilty of the body and blood of the Lord' means, I think, that we eat without loving those whom Christ loved and died for, and with whom we are eating the meal. Because, if we do not love them, we cannot love him, and if we do not love him, we will not love them. Why does Paul begin his account of the institution with the phrase, 'The Lord Jesus, *in the night that he was betrayed*, took bread ...'? He quietly reminds the Corinthians of Judas, who certainly was 'guilty of the body and blood of the Lord'. And so, quietly but firmly, he tells them that they too will betray Jesus, just as completely as Judas, if they eat and drink without 'discerning the body' – in both senses.

So he encourages them to test themselves as preparation for eating and drinking (11:28). I do not think that this means prolonged heart-searching and introspection. It means examining ourselves in the light of his particular challenge in this passage. What is the quality of our love for each other? Are we truly committed to each other, as to Christ? Are there any quarrels that need to be patched up? We are reminded of the teaching of Jesus: 'If you are bringing your gift to the altar and there remember that your brother or sister has a quarrel with you, leave your gift there before the altar, and go. First be reconciled with your brother or sister, and then come and offer your gift' (Matt. 5:23f.). Reconciliation takes priority over worship! Paul would say: because worship is *impossible* without it, and the Lord's Supper is *dangerous* without it.

Before we draw some conclusions, there are three more points to be considered from Paul's teaching, all drawing on a verse we have not looked at, 11:26: 'As often as you eat this bread and drink this cup, you proclaim the Lord's death until he comes'.

First, he too (like Jesus) thinks of the Eucharist as looking in two directions, both back to the cross and forward to the Kingdom, the coming of the Lord. The Eucharist celebrates *both* comings of the Lord.

Secondly, Paul draws out an aspect of the Eucharist which was implicit in Jesus' treatment of

Passover – its *public nature*. Passover was not a secret festival. Many other religions had hidden rites and ceremonies, the details of which were only revealed to members, under strict conditions of secrecy. Judaism had no secrets like that! Passover was a massive event, and the details of it and its meaning were publicly available to all who wanted to know.

Similarly Paul says that, in the Eucharist, we 'proclaim' the Lord's death. This does not mean that we deliberately make it a kind of show. Rather, it means that we are ready to be very open about the message it expresses – which is, after all, the wonderful gospel of the love of God in Christ. To take part in the Eucharist means 'proclaiming the Lord's death' by our participation, and this in turn means being ready to talk about it elsewhere as well. The church that *feeds* is the church that *speaks* – of the double coming of the Lord.

And thirdly, does Paul make a recommendation here about the frequency with which we should celebrate it? 'As often as you eat this bread ...'. Passover took place only once a year, but clearly the church in Corinth was celebrating the Lord's Supper quite frequently. The implication of 11:17-20 is that they were doing it every time they met for worship. Actually, Paul's expression is quite open. 'As often as' does not imply any particular frequency. We do not know whether he approved the Corinthian pattern or not – although they probably learned it from him originally. It appears from Acts 20:7 that the church in Troas did it weekly with Paul's encouragement. But at the moment, he clearly wishes that the Corinthians were not doing it so often!

Let us now draw some conclusions from Paul's teaching for ourselves, thinking back to the questions with which we started Part Two (see above, page 55). Four things emerge powerfully from Paul:

(1) *Eating the bread and wine means a very real participation in the body and blood of Christ* – just as real (though completely different) as the 'fellowship' with demons which idolatry creates. Not long ago a missionary friend described to me the horrible, demonic character of some of the festivals she had witnessed in temples in India. To her and her colleagues, no proof was needed that the devil was in charge. Paul and the Corinthians knew this too. They had experienced it first-hand. They knew that 'powers' were at work in the temples in Corinth, powers which had bound them into a lifestyle of sexual perversion, theft and drunkenness (see 1 Cor. 6:9-11): 'but you were washed, you were sanctified, you were justified in the name of our Lord Jesus Christ and in the Spirit of our God!' (6:11).

Now they must glorify God in their bodies, which are 'temples of the Holy Spirit' (6:19f.), just as they as a church together are 'the temple of God, because the Spirit of God dwells in you' (3:16). The worship which is offered in this temple will involve just as much intimate contact with the deity they serve, as ever they 'enjoyed' in the pagan temples of Corinth. And at the heart of this worship is the Eucharist, in which the cup and the bread are 'fellowship' in the blood and body of Christ.

I do not believe that Paul's thinking about the Eucharist was just shaped by the negative analogy of pagan idolatry. We will explore in the next chapter the positive motivations and reasons behind his teaching. But it seems clear that, for Paul, the Eucharist is the occasion of a unique kind of 'fellowship' with Christ, when our union with him and with each other is uniquely celebrated and strengthened. 'We who are many are one bread, one body, for we all partake of the one bread' (10:17).

How would he reply if we pinned Paul down with the question, 'Do you believe that a change occurs in the bread and wine?' I do not think we yet know enough about his thinking to define his answer. Anticipating the next chapter, I think he would say, 'Yes – but they are still very firmly bread and wine!'

(2) *There is not a hint of 'priestly presidency' in Paul's presentation.* As we saw above, the formal structure of the Eucharist seems to be a matter of total indifference to him. He is far more concerned about the moral and spiritual unity of the church in

worship, than about what words are used or who leads.

This comes out in both halves of 1 Corinthians 11 – both in the difficult first section about men and women in worship (11:2-16), and in the section on the Eucharist. Though hard to interpret, 11:2-16 is all about conduct in worship. Paul is clearly concerned about the disorder in the Corinthian church. But the antidote to disorder is not *proper structures* – the right words, the right leadership – but *proper relationships*, rightly understanding the respective roles of men and women in worship.

Similarly in 11:17-34 the answer to the grave problems at the Eucharist is not structural, but relational. The Corinthians must sort out their relationships with each other. The implication is that once the relationships are in order, then the Eucharist really *will* be the Supper of the Lord! There is not a hint that, of course, they would then need to address the further, formal problem of having one ordained by Paul to lead the service. 1 Corinthians 14:26-33 shows us what the style of Corinthian worship was. And the order he there encourages is again not structural, but practical. They must not all speak at once! They must act together as a body.

(3) *Paul lays overwhelming emphasis on the importance of fellowship expressed in the Eucharist.* This we have seen very clearly in our study. It is something which, I believe, many churches have gravely neglected, including my own – although it

is encouraging to see signs of a renewal both of understanding and of practice here. In recent years many churches have rediscovered eucharistic togetherness. And some Roman Catholic writers have strongly emphasised the Eucharist as the fellowship meal of the local church. This is fascinating, since in the 16th century only the Reformers were saying this (and only *some* of them!).

But Paul said it long before. We cannot grasp Christ's body in the sacrament, without grasping Christ's body in the church. That says it all! And it is the example of Jesus' self-sacrifice for us, celebrated in the Eucharist, which provides the model for our fellowship as a church.

I was very moved on one occasion when I found myself administering the bread and wine to two people kneeling side-by-side at the Communion rail: first, the chairman of a South American bank, a very wealthy and influential man; next to him, a woman who spent much of her week cleaning the houses of the wealthy in the village. Both knelt, equal in their need, equal in their trust in Christ, and equally members of his body. What a powerful witness to the reality of Christ and to his power to break down barriers! In a recent book Dr Kwame Bediako, a leading African theologian, points out how important the Lord's Supper is for showing the world how the national barriers between people have been abolished in Christ. In a world torn by nationalism, this is a message desperately needed.

(4) *Paul points us towards the importance of preparation for participation.* We need to take seriously what he says about the danger of receiving the bread and wine unworthily. But we must not exaggerate what he says so much that it clouds our participation with fear. The Lord invites *sinners* to his table – sinners just like us, whose love and fellowship are gravely imperfect. The danger is not our sinfulness, but 'not discerning the body' – not *caring* about our fellowship with each other and with Christ, treating both him and our fellow-Christians with disregard and without joy. This is what preparation needs to focus on. Are there any breaches of fellowship that need to be healed? Are there any gifts that I can or should give to my brothers or sisters in Christ? Do they have any needs that I could meet?

The word Paul uses in 11:28 means 'test' rather than 'examine'. We need to eat and drink in the context of putting our love to the test. He puts it vividly in 1 Corinthians 5:7f., where he tells them to 'clear out the yeast of wickedness' and to 'celebrate the feast' (the Passover-Eucharist) 'with the unleavened bread of sincerity and truth'.

We have now looked at all the main 'Eucharist' passages in the New Testament. But there is more biblical material yet to examine – material which I believe greatly helps us to understand how it was possible for Paul to link fellowship with Christ specifically to eating and drinking the bread and wine of the Eucharist. And the same material will help all the churches forward, if we can agree that this is how the Bible teaches us to understand the Lord's Supper.

# 9. The Eucharist – a 'Prophetic Sign'?

It would be good to say at the outset what this chapter is going to suggest and argue for. It is that the breaking and provision of the bread and wine in the Eucharist is a *prophetic sign*, given by God and administered by the church, which promises fellowship with Christ to all who eat and drink with faith. I am using 'prophetic sign' in a technical sense, the sense in which it is used to describe various symbolic or significant acts by prophets in the Bible. I shall illustrate what I mean below!

Describing the Eucharist as a 'sign' has a long pedigree. For instance, Article 25 of the 39 Articles of the Church of England describes sacraments as 'sure witnesses, and effectual signs of grace and God's good will towards us, by the which he doth work invisibly in us'.

Similarly the Westminster Confession of Faith says that 'sacraments are holy signs and seals of the covenant of grace, immediately instituted by God, to represent Christ and his benefits, and to confirm our interest in him' (27:1). Then it goes on to describe baptism as a 'sign and seal of the covenant of grace' (28:1).

The Reformers often referred to the Eucharist, or specifically to the bread and wine, as 'signs', and indeed the words 'sacrament' and 'sign' sometimes seem interchangeable for them.

Recently it is fascinating to see this word appearing amongst Roman Catholic writers on the Eucharist. As I mentioned in Part One, the term 'transubstantiation' has been largely dropped by Catholic theologians today, although of course it is still officially a dogma of the church. Instead, the word 'transignification' has appeared, to describe what happens to the bread and wine in the Eucharist. They do not change materially, this view maintains, but they take on a new nature as 'signs' from God of something vital in his relationship to us. Just as a piece of cloth 'becomes' something else when it is made into a flag, or a cup of tea and a biscuit 'become' a warm expression of friendship, so the bread and wine 'become' signs of his grace towards us.

This is fine, but it is sometimes left unclear what *makes* the bread and wine 'signs' of God's grace. Does *God* do something to them, to make them into 'signs'? If so, what does he do to them? Or do *we* make them into signs, by setting them apart in the service? If *we* do it, then are we saying anything more than Zwingli said 400 years ago – to the horror of the Roman Catholic Church?

I believe that the biblical understanding of 'prophetic signs' helps us greatly here, and that there are good biblical reasons for thinking of the Eucharist, and of baptism, as prophetic signs. The argument builds up by stages, as follows:

*Stage One: a general look at biblical prophets*
'Prophetic sign' is not a biblical expression, but it describes a biblical phenomenon. In fact, it was one of the regular marks of prophets in the Bible that they performed 'signs' of various types. And always, the sign was meant to incorporate and express a word from God. This might have been something the prophet had already directly said, or the sign might be left unexplained. People would see it, and be puzzled, and try to work out what it meant.

This needs illustrating. The most obvious kind of prophetic sign was a significant gesture of some kind. Ahijah the prophet met Jeroboam, the future king of Israel, who at that stage had no notions of becoming king, and tore his (new!) cloak into twelve pieces, ten of which he gave to Jeroboam, telling him that God intended to give him ten of the twelve tribes of Israel to rule over (1 Kings 11:29ff.). Jeremiah solemnly broke a pot in front of the elders of Israel, telling them that God was going to smash the nation (Jer. 19). Agabus took Paul's belt from him and tied himself up with it, signifying that Paul would be imprisoned in Jerusalem (Acts 21:10f.).

In all these cases the sign was accompanied by explanatory words. The point about the sign was

not that it just *illustrated* the words vividly. The
action of performing the sign was *itself* a word from
God, something with its own power. This is seen
clearly in 2 Kings 13:14-19, where it is not the
prophet but someone else who performs the sign.
When Jehoash shoots the arrow, Elisha declares,
'The LORD's arrow of victory, the arrow of victory
over Aram!' (13:17). Then, because Jehoash only
strikes the ground three times with the arrows, he
limits the word of God to him. Elisha tells him,
'You should have struck the ground five or six
times! Then you would have defeated Aram and
completely destroyed it' (13:19).

We must remember this every time we meet a
prophetic sign in the Bible. For three years Isaiah
had to walk around virtually naked. People must
have asked what this meant. The word was spoken
by the action. For whom was it intended? Then
came the explanation, 'Just as my servant Isaiah
has gone stripped and barefoot for three years, as a
sign and portent against Egypt and Cush, so the
king of Assyria will lead away the Egyptian cap-
tives and Cushite exiles ...' (Is. 20:3f.).

Similarly Ezekiel had to perform some extraordinary actions which were not immediately explained. He had to lie on one side for 390 days in
front of a model of Jerusalem under siege (Ezek. 4),
and then he had to shave off all his hair, divide it
into thirds and do different things with each part
(Ezek. 5). Later we read that, in front of an audi-

ence, he had to pack up his belongings, then dig a hole through the wall of his house and carry them all out. We gather that people asked him, 'What are you doing?' When a prophet started doing things like this, people took notice. When God allowed him to reply (the next day), he said, 'I am a sign to you. As I have done, so it will be done to them' (referring to the inhabitants of Jerusalem: Ezekiel 12:11).

Perhaps the most vivid Old Testament example is that of Hosea, who had to marry a prostitute, give his children extraordinary names, and then go and buy back his wife when she was unfaithful to him (Hosea 1-3).

*All these prophetic actions were in themselves powerful 'words' from God.* Of course, they did not compel a response from people. They did nothing magical to those who witnessed them, though they could have a powerful effect if people believed them and acted upon them. Jeroboam believed the word of Ahijah, and so he seized the opportunity to become king when it presented itself (1 Kings 12:1f.). Jeremiah's sign with the pot was strongly rejected by Passhur the priest, who had poor Jeremiah flogged and put in the stocks – and got another prophetic word as a result (Jer. 20:1-6).

What is the relevance of all this to the Eucharist? The argument develops:

*Stage Two: a look at John the Baptist and at Paul*
John the Baptist performed prophetic signs in this
biblical tradition. Actually his appearance constituted a sign, for he deliberately dressed like Elijah
(Matt. 3:4; 2 Kings 1:8). If people thought about his
peculiar appearance, they might have been reminded of the prophecy of Malachi 4:5. But su-
premely *his baptism* was such a sign. It had paral-
lels with the various ritual washings which Jews
used to perform, but John was not inviting people
simply to a ritual washing. It was something much
more *sign*ificant. His was a 'baptism of repentance,
for the forgiveness of sins' (Luke 3:3).

We realise the true significance of John's baptism when we reflect on what he did *not* tell people
to do. Normally, repentance would be marked by
making some form of appropriate restitution for the
sin committed, and/or by offering a sacrifice in
Jerusalem. John sets these requirements aside. He
simply offers people forgiveness if they repent,
signified vividly by baptism. The act of baptism
itself thus expressed the prophetic 'word' – the
direct, unconditional assurance of forgiveness by
God. No wonder John offended the establishment
(Matt. 21:25f., 31f.)! He was effectively undermin-
ing the whole religious system of Judean Judaism,
by prophetic authority. Forgiveness was now available directly from God, bypassing the temple in
Jerusalem and all that it stood for.

Explosive stuff! But then it always was the lot of

prophets to undermine the *status quo*.

There is a direct line of development between the baptism of John and Christian baptism. They are not the same thing, as we see clearly from the story in Acts 19:1-7: in Ephesus Paul met some disciples of John the Baptist, and when he discovered that they had never received the Holy Spirit, he pointed them to Jesus, to whom John had borne witness. 'When they heard Paul, they were baptised in the name of Jesus, and when Paul laid his hands on them the Holy Spirit came upon them, and they began to speak in tongues and prophesy' (Acts 19:5f.).

Christian baptism is not *less* than the baptism of John, it is *greater* than it. But it has the same quality as a 'prophetic word'. It promises, not just forgiveness, but the gift of the Holy Spirit to all who believe – just as John had prophesied: 'someone greater than me is coming soon! I am not worthy to bend and remove his shoes. I baptise you with water, but he will baptise you with the Holy Spirit!' (Mark 1:7f.).

The relationship between water-baptism and Spirit-baptism has long puzzled Christians and caused disagreement. We will not get involved with that problem in detail now, because I simply want to point a way forward: isn't it helpful to think of baptism as a *prophetic sign*? It seems to be how Paul thinks of it in Romans 6:3f.: 'Don't you know that all of us, who have been baptised into Christ,

were baptised into his *death*? So we were *buried*
with him, through baptism into his death, so that we
might live a renewed life, just as Christ was raised
from the dead by the Father's glory'.

How can Paul say that we were joined to Christ
'through' baptism? He cannot mean that we were
put into Christ *by* our baptism, as if baptism was the
syringe that injected us into him. For Paul, we are
joined to Christ by *faith*, and that alone (e.g. Romans 5:1f.). But why then does he use that word
'through'? I think the best answer is that he is
thinking of Christian baptism on the model of the
baptism of John. Those who responded to John's
call received the forgiveness of their sins *through*
their baptism by him, because that was the prophetic 'word' which assured them that their repentance was accepted. Similarly, baptism is the solid
*word from God* which assures us that we who
believe are joined to Christ who saves.

An objection to this might be that prophetic
signs have to be administered by prophets – don't
they? How then can baptism be a prophetic sign,
when any Christian, not just 'prophets', could
administer it? The answer to this is not hard. By
pouring out his Holy Spirit onto the church at
Pentecost, God has given *the church as a whole* a
prophetic ministry. In the Bible, the Holy Spirit is
first and foremost *the Spirit of prophecy* – that is, he
equips and empowers the church to speak and to
minister in God's name in the world. When Jesus

breathed on his disciples and gave them the Spirit, he even told them that they had authority to forgive or retain sins (John 20:22f.) – meaning, I think, that we have the power of life and death over the world because of the precious gospel which we administer in his name. Baptism signals joining the company which belongs to Christ – and therefore it is basically an *act of the church*, something given to us by God to do in his name to all who believe.

And so it is very appropriate to think of baptism as a prophetic sign in this biblical sense. The argument moves on:

*Stage Three: a look at Jesus himself*
Did Jesus perform prophetic signs? Yes, he most certainly did. This is the best way to understand his miracles, as well as several other 'significant' actions of his. Some of the Old Testament prophetic signs were miraculous, especially those associated with Elisha. Now, with the coming of Jesus, miraculous signs burst onto the scene again.

It is particularly John's Gospel which draws out the 'sign' element of Jesus' miracles. 'Sign' is John's favourite description of them (e.g. 2:11; 6:2). And John tries to make sure that his readers are able to understand the signs, that is, that they can grasp the implicit message or word from God which each sign contains and conveys. For instance, he spends much longer than the other Gospels telling the story of the feeding of the five thousand, because he records the accompanying teaching of Jesus about the Bread of Life (John 6). Some of those who saw it thought that the sign meant that Jesus was the Prophet like Moses, promised in Deuteronomy 18:15, so they tried to make Jesus king (John 6:14f.). John quietly explains that this is the wrong interpretation. Yes, Jesus fulfils Deuteronomy 18, but he is not going to be a political deliverer like Moses. He is going to save people from death by being the Bread of Life.

Other actions performed by Jesus may helpfully be described as prophetic signs. At the end of chapter 7, I mentioned his riding on a donkey into Jerusalem, his cursing of the fig tree, and his cleansing of the temple. These are all actions of a prophetic nature, incorporating a powerful 'word' in themselves. We could also think of simpler actions, like touching the leper (Mark 1:41). This was not just an expression of compassion. People were forbidden to touch lepers, for fear of contracting the ritual 'uncleanness' that went with the disease. So when the leper said to Jesus, 'If you will, you can cleanse me' (Mark 1:40), he was not just asking for healing from a disfiguring skin condition. He was asking for ritual 'cleansing' and the restoration to the community which would follow.

So when Jesus touched the leper, and said 'I will – be clean', and the leprosy vanished, this was a *dramatic prophetic action*: instead of Jesus being made unclean by the touch, the leper is cleansed.

Impurity is pushed back, rather than being extended, by this touch! The action speaks volumes about Jesus, and his ministry, and the new thing that God is doing with the coming of the Kingdom.

I concluded our look at Jesus' institution of the Eucharist in chapter 7 (before the summary and conclusions) with the thought that Jesus' actions at the Last Supper were prophetic. In the context of a ministry full of such actions, this is the best way to understand them. The actions of taking the bread and wine of the Passover, and transforming their significance with those dramatic words, were 'prophetic' in this sense in which we have seen it throughout the Bible. They were actions loaded with a word from God. 'This is my body ... This is my blood of the covenant which is being poured out for many, for the forgiveness of sins' (Matt. 26:26,28). From this moment onwards, Passover can never be the same for all who accept that Jesus speaks and acts from God.

But what did these actions signify? As so often with prophetic signs, I think that those who heard and saw (in this case the disciples) must have been totally bemused. Only after his death and resurrection, these words at the Last Supper must have come back to them, and helped them to understand what had happened on the cross. *His* blood shed for them, not that of the Passover lamb ... And they must have reflected too on the invitation to *eat* his body and *drink* his blood. He had not just turned the bread and wine into symbols. They had then eaten them.

I wonder whether their minds went back to some other words of Jesus, which likewise they must have failed to understand at the time. Once again John helps us by recording them. They are the words with which Jesus explained the meaning of the feeding of the five thousand. At the time, his words were not only puzzling, but also shocking to Jews brought up with an absolute prohibition on drinking blood (see Leviticus 17:10-14): 'Truly truly I say to you, unless you eat the flesh of the Son of man, and drink his blood, you do not have life within you. Anyone who eats my flesh and drinks my blood has eternal life, and I will raise that person up at the last day. For my flesh is real food, and my blood is real drink' (John 6:53-55).

But now those words spring to life! Jesus invites them to eat his flesh and drink his blood, not *literally*, but under a *sign*, as they celebrate Passover in memory of him. One of the things John remembered about those strange words of Jesus was that he spoke them in connection with a forthcoming Passover (John 6:4).

Can we take this line of thought a little further? Did those first disciples believe that, every time they obeyed Jesus' command to 'do this in remembrance of me', and celebrated Passover in remembrance of him rather than of the Exodus, the bread and the wine took on that same quality as a pro-

phetic sign from God? It seems highly likely that
they did.

*Stage Four: The Eucharist as a prophetic sign*
I find it most helpful to apply this line of thought to
the Eucharist. This gives us the answer, I believe, to
the vexed question, 'What actually happens to the
bread and wine? And how does eating them do us
good?' We should follow the lead of those who
describe the sacraments as 'signs', but we should
fill out the meaning of the word 'sign' with its true,
biblical content.

We saw above that, for Paul, the Eucharist is
more than just a visual aid reminding us of Jesus'
death. It is 'spiritual food' and 'spiritual drink' (1
Cor. 10:3f.), and it is 'the table of the Lord' (1 Cor.
10:21), at which we experience 'fellowship' in his
body and his blood (1 Cor. 10:16). How can he
make such a close connection between these physical things, bread and wine, and the Lord who is
Spirit? The answer is that the Lord, who is Spirit,
communicates himself in and through these things,
just as he does throughout the Bible whenever he
'embodies' his word and his power in a physical
sign.

Paul compares baptism and the Eucharist to the
Exodus experiences Israel went through. 'They
were all baptised into Moses in the cloud and in the
sea', he says (1 Cor. 10:2). 'And they all ate the
same spiritual food, and all drank the same spiritual

drink, for they drank from the spiritual rock which
was following them: and that rock was the Christ!'
(1 Cor. 10:3f.). Moses was the greatest prophet in
the Old Testament, and he too performed remarkable signs which expressed God's commitment to
save his people. He stretched out his hand over the
Red Sea, and the waters parted to let Israel through
(Exod. 14:21f.). When they ran out of food, he
prayed and God provided manna (Exod. 16). He
struck the rock with his staff, and God made water
flow out of it as a sign of his presence with Israel
(Exod. 17:5-7).

Paul takes these stories as pictures ('types', 1
Cor. 10:6) of the provision that God makes for us,
now, in baptism and the Eucharist. Those physical
objects, the manna and the water, nourished Israel
physically, but also expressed God's determination to support and sustain them, and to maintain
his relationship with them – the *covenant*. Paul
brings out that thought with his dramatic comment,
'the rock was the Christ!' By this, he means (I
believe) that the water-providing rock was the
*Messiah* to Israel then, God's anointed means of
saving Israel, of making and keeping them his
people in the wilderness.

But by calling the rock 'the Christ', Paul makes
the parallel with the Eucharist so vivid! In the
Eucharist (as in baptism), God expresses his commitment to save us, to sustain us through our
wilderness wanderings, and to nourish us by com-

municating *his Christ* to us. His Christ is not now a rock, but the glorious person of our Lord Jesus Christ, and the food and drink are not manna and water, but the bread we break and the cup we drink at his table in fellowship with him. The signs are different, but signs they still are, speaking with as much power to us now as the manna and the water spoke to Israel of old.

There is a difference, of course. The manna and water just appeared, direct from God. The bread and wine, on the other hand, are provided by us, and the actions of breaking and distributing are performed by us. But this helps us with another question which has long puzzled and divided the church: is it right to think of the Eucharist as an *offering* or *sacrifice*? As we have seen, the word 'offer' was used nearly from the beginning (see the prayer of Hippolytus at the end of chapter 16), and gradually people came to think of the Eucharist as a *sacrifice* like that of Jesus himself.

The Passover origin of the Eucharist makes it wrong to think of the Eucharist as a *sacrifice for sin*, as we have seen. But it is certainly appropriate to offer the bread and the cup to God, because we want him to take them and make them into prophetic signs that speak powerfully, like the manna and water. We cannot do that – only he can. And so we give them to him, praying that he will.

There is nothing magical or automatic about the blessing we receive from partaking. Paul's purpose in 1 Corinthians 10 is in fact to *warn* the Corinthians: in spite of these great blessings for Israel, 'God was not pleased with most of them, for we read that their bodies lay scattered in the desert. These things took place as types for us, so that we may not set our hearts on evil, as they did' (10:5f.). Then Paul lists the 'evils' on which the Israelites set their hearts – idolatry (7), sexual immorality (8), hostile distrust of God (9), grumbling and discontent (10). *All these things will still rob us of the blessing promised to us in the Eucharist*, because we cannot have fellowship with Christ if our hearts are bound up in these sins. As with all prophetic signs, the blessing comes to those who believe them and respond in that faith.

Paul is fearful that the Corinthians' response is totally inadequate. They do not 'discern the body' as they should, and so are in danger of 'eating and drinking judgment' upon themselves (11:29). We thought above about what Paul means by this. Here, we can add the thought that *to treat the Eucharist flippantly and thoughtlessly, like the Corinthians, is to throw God's word back in his face – a word which he can only speak to us at great cost, because he gave his Son to die for us*. Just as Passhur the priest came under judgment for rejecting Jeremiah's sign with the pot (see Jer. 20:1-6), so will we, if we do not receive the bread and wine *as a word from God to sinners who delight to belong to the body of his Son*.

But what a blessing when we do receive them like that! In Part Three, we will think of some practical guidelines for receiving communion. Before we turn to that, however, I want to close Part Two by commenting on the way in which this understanding of the Eucharist solves the questions we raised in Part One, especially the *theoretical* questions about what actually happens in the Eucharist.

I really believe that all the various Christian traditions could unite around this understanding of the Eucharist. This is, after all, the *biblical* understanding of it, and if we cannot unite around that, then woe betide us. Nothing has been taken away from the *receptionist* tradition, which wants to emphasise that the blessing comes to us as we rightly remember the Lord. Nothing has been taken away from the *realist* tradition except the literal, physical interpretation associated with 'transubstantiation'. Nothing has been taken away from the *symbolic* and *corporate* traditions. They all contribute vital insights, which are gathered up and joined in this comprehensive, biblical understanding:

* Yes, the bread and wine *really* become something different in the Eucharist: they become a prophetic vehicle to us of the grace and power of God, an assurance *from him* of his love and forgiveness in Christ.

* Yes, the benefit *does* all depend upon the quality of our obedience to the command to 'do this in remembrance of me'. There is nothing automatic about it. 'Fellowship' takes place both in the eating, and in our hearts, as we eat with love and faith towards Christ. If our hearts are not right with him, then we must hear Paul's warning.

* Yes, we may rightly call the bread and wine *symbols* of the body and blood of Christ. We eat them *as if we* were eating his very flesh. And they become symbols both because *we* set them apart, as his church, and because *God* sets them apart for us. Our action and God's action come together, because the church is empowered to *act prophetically on God's behalf* in doing this.

* And Yes, we must affirm the vital importance of our *corporate* reception of this word from God. The Israelites received the manna and the water, not as gifts to each of them individually, but as gifts to the whole people, expressions of God's covenant with Israel. So we are *joined to each other* by our common feeding upon Christ, who was given once for *all* of us, and brings in 'the new covenant in my blood'.

It is my prayer that this book may serve a little to draw the churches together around this biblical understanding of the Eucharist.

# Part Three:
# Feasting with the Lord

This third part of the book is devoted to giving some guidance about *enjoying* the Eucharist. The word 'enjoy' is important. Of course I do not mean that the Eucharist is somehow meant to *entertain* us. We do not go to the Eucharist for the same purpose as the theatre or the cinema. But we should enjoy it, nonetheless - just as we should enjoy *God*. The enjoyment comes from *the company we keep* at this celebration.

That is why I have entitled this part 'Feasting with the Lord'. Just as we enjoy a meal with close friends, because we relax and feel completely at home in their company, so we can enjoy eating with the Lord our Saviour. The Eucharist is different from a dinner-party, naturally – but only because the Lord with whom we eat is different from all other friends.

One of the chief differences is that we do not only feast *with* him, but we also feast *on* him. But thinking of it as a dinner-party with friends still helps us to understand this. When we eat with friends, we are not only nourished by the food on the table. We also feed upon their company, and come away refreshed by it. The personal communion with them is a vital part of the 'nourishment' we derive from the dinner. So in a sense, we feast *on* them, as well as *with* them.

So it is with the Eucharist. If it is a 'sign' to us, expressing Christ's commitment to us in giving himself for us on the cross (see chapter 9), then he is the host at this meal-table. These 'prophetic signs' come from him, and we receive them from his hand. He is present with us, not just because he gives these signs, but also because *they are signs of his presence*. Understood in the biblical way I have outlined in Part Two, the bread and the wine not only *picture* his self-giving for us on the cross, but also *communicate* him to us: they embody a word from him to us, saying, 'Here I am, given for you'. So we feast both with him and on him, enjoying his presence in this unique way.

A dinner-party with friends cements friendship. By being there, and joining in the fun, we let our friends know how much we value them, and express our commitment to them. Again, it is the same with the Eucharist. By accepting the invitation, and joining in, we tell the Lord how much we value his friendship and his gift of himself to us, and we express our commitment to him, and to all the others at the Feast.

This kind of enjoyment is not without pain. It is a *deep* joy, the joy that comes from facing up to sin, and sorrow, and suffering, and finding the answer to them in the sufferings of the Lord we meet. It is the joy of Jesus himself, 'who, for the joy that was set before him, endured the cross, despising the shame, and is seated at the right hand of God' (Heb. 12:2). This is the joy that comes from standing alongside others in *their* weakness and pain, and from being realistic about *our* weakness and pain, and from knowing that *his* weakness and pain is our salvation. It is unique! Let us not miss out.

What follows is a guide to enjoying the Eucharist. It builds on Parts One and Two, but stands on its own as well. There are seven brief chapters here, covering different aspects of preparing for it and then participating, and finishing with a selection of some of the best Communion hymns available today – to provide a resource for preparation, or for use during the quiet moments of the service.

# 10. Accepting your invitation

How should we prepare for the Eucharist? There is no standard answer to this question, because the churches all have such different patterns for celebrating it, and many of them give particular guidance about preparation. For instance, some Catholic traditions recommend attending Confession, and suggest fasting beforehand. Fasting is required by the Orthodox churches – a minimum of two days' abstention from meat, fish, wine, oil, and all animal products. Some Presbyterian churches have an elaborate programme of visitation by the church elders before Communion. Other churches – like the Anglican – are content to regard the first part of the service as preparation for the Communion which follows. The sheer variety of different practices leads me to my first comment:

(1) *It is vital that you are happy to conform to the practice of the church you belong to, whatever it is*. This is vital to the *fellowship* which you will experience and express by participating. Whatever recommendations your church makes about preparation, follow them happily if you can.

This actually applies not just to preparation, but to the whole conduct of the service. Sometimes, for the sake of fellowship, you will have to put up with things which you yourself do not like. Maybe you do not like the style of music generally employed in your church. Or perhaps the minister's voice grates on your ears. Perhaps you do not enjoy children being present – or wish that they were present. You could even have more fundamental doubts about the rightness of the way your church celebrates the Eucharist. *These things must not get in the way of your 'enjoyment' of the Feast.* You may need to prepare yourself ahead of the event, to make sure that you can cope.

I find myself in this kind of situation at the moment. Last year the church where I worship took the decision to stop using a common cup, and bought individual glasses which are served to the congregation in specially designed trays. (This is the custom in many Baptist churches.) Personally, I find that these individual cups fight against the symbolism of the single 'cup of blessing'. As we saw above, Jesus changed the Passover meal by giving *his* cup to all the disciples, so that they did not drink from their own. But I *must* not let this conviction of mine spoil my 'enjoyment' of the meal. I must gladly support the practice of my church, for the sake of fellowship. (Indeed, I must accept responsibility for it: I am one of the church elders who recommended the change! All in all, it was the right thing to do.)

If you have a difficulty of this kind with your

church, you must come to terms with it in your heart
before you participate. Talk to your minister or
priest, if necessary, or to a close friend. If this kind
of adjustment is vital to fellowship, then my second
comment about preparation is even more vital:

(2) *Make sure that you are at 'peace' with all
others in your church.* We saw in Part Two how
much emphasis Paul laid on this, in writing to the
church in Corinth. He believed that *they could not
celebrate the Eucharist at all*, while not at peace
with each other. They went through the motions,
but 'you do not eat the Lord's Supper, when you
gather' (1 Cor. 11:20). This is easier said than done,
but it is crucial to our 'enjoyment'.

If you know that there is 'something' between
you and someone else in the church – some unresolved conflict, unforgiven sin, old resentment –
then do your best to sort it out. This may be very
difficult to do. You may need to ask for someone's
forgiveness, at great cost to your pride.

But remember that we come to the Feast as
sinners. What makes it 'not the Lord's Supper' is
*lack of desire* for reconciliation. That was the
problem in Corinth: they were basically *glad* about
being opposed to each other (1 Cor. 1:12). This is
important to remember, in the case of conflicts
which cannot be resolved just by a few quiet words.
One of the parties may not be aware that they have
given deep offence, and it may simply not be right
or wise to mention it to them. Or there may be a

personality clash which goes back years, and which cannot be sorted out over a cup of tea. In such cases we come to the Feast facing our weakness, with regret for our failures, desiring a new start, and looking to the Lord for his forgiveness, his wisdom and his power.

Preparation in such cases might involve asking yourself what you can do to serve the other person concerned. Is there some way in which you could minister to them, meet one of their needs? It could be something practical, or a card with a loving message, or just a heartfelt prayer if at the moment nothing else is possible. This was what was missing in Corinth, because the rich members of the church were simply forgetting the needs of the poor. You need not undertake such a ministry *before* coming to the Feast, but make sure you do it afterwards, if God has prompted you to think of it.

Many churches have a moment in the service called 'The Peace'. We will think more about this below. Generally, people exchange a warm hand-shake with some words like 'The peace of the Lord be with you'. Even if this does not feature in your church, imagine that it does. Could you do this, genuinely and from the heart, with everyone who belongs to your church? If the answer is, 'With everyone *except* Mr X / Ms Y', then you have some work to do. You may not be able to sort out the difficulty with them, whatever it is. It may remain unresolved, for the moment. But you need to get to

the point in your own heart where (by God's grace)
you reply 'With everyone *especially* Mr X / Ms Y'.

My final comment about preparation is simply:
(3) *Make sure you look forward to being there.* Do
not let it become just a matter of routine. This is a
danger, particularly for those who belong to
churches where it is the central, weekly act of
worship. Take steps to make sure that it does not
lose its sparkle for you. Don't just be a passenger.
Grasp the service, make it your act of worship. The
hymns provided at the end of this book may help!

# 11. Listening to your host

A dinner-guest who talks nonstop about himself or herself basically ruins the occasion. They draw everyone's attention onto themselves: look at me, listen to me, sympathise with my problems! They highjack the dinner and turn it into an ego-trip.

It is horribly possible for us to do this with the Eucharist. Of course, the Lord *invites* us to come with our weaknesses and woes. We *must* not leave them in the church lobby. He wants the real you and me at his table, not some pseudo-religious cardboard imitation. But he wants us there so that *he* can give *himself* to us. And he cannot do that, unless we are ready to turn our attention away from ourselves and to *listen to him*.

This is something we can do throughout the service. In all churches without exception, I think, the Eucharist is usually part of a wider service which includes Bible-reading and almost always a sermon. On most occasions, this Bible-reading (and sermon) *precedes* the Eucharist. This is a wonderful opportunity to listen to our host! At the table he will speak that powerful, prophetic word through which he will communicate himself to us. Before we gather there, we have an opportunity to hear him speak through his written Word, the Bible.

The churches in the Reformation tradition have all emphasised this *unity of Word and sacrament*. Originally, this emphasis was a reaction against the Mediaeval Catholic practices of solitary Masses, and of Latin Masses which contained no sermon in the language of the people. But the modern Catholic liturgies are now very different, and recognise that the ministry of the Word is vital for us as we meet at the table of the Lord.

In churches where a regular pattern of readings is followed, you might find it helpful to read the set passages ahead of the service, as preparation for it. Hopefully, the sermon will help you to apply their message to yourself. Above all, come to the service *expecting* God to speak to you – whether through the readings, or through the sermon, or through the prayers, or the singing, or the Feasting, or a conversation afterwards. He may want you to grasp some truth more clearly, or to catch a fresh glimpse of the depth of his love for you, or he may want to point out a sin or problem in your life that needs attention.

Whatever his particular desire for you, *you know that he will speak to you at every Eucharist* – because every Eucharist will include that 'word' of love and acceptance in the bread and the wine. And if the whole service is thus about God speaking to us, then we need to have our ears open throughout, to hear whatever particular things he may want to say to us as well.

As we saw in Part One, it was their emphasis on

the unity of Word and sacrament which led the Reformation churches to keep an ordained minister in charge of the Eucharist. Even though they believed in 'the priesthood of all believers', they did not want any Tom, Dick or Harry leading the service, because Tom, Dick and Harry might have some very odd ideas to peddle. Only churches in the Baptist tradition, and eventually others like the Plymouth Brethren, have allowed anyone in the congregation to lead the Eucharist. The Brethren retain a consistent connection between Word and sacrament by also allowing anyone to minister the Word, as prompted by the Spirit.

Once again, we need to rejoice in the variety that exists in the churches, rather than insist on the rightness of our own church's practice. As we saw in Part Two, Jesus told *his disciples* to celebrate Passover in remembrance of him – they were to do it *together*; and Paul does not fix any rules about the leadership of the Eucharist in Corinth. Personally, I feel that it is *appropriate* if the one who leads the church in celebrating the Eucharist has also been set apart to teach and to lead the church. This expresses the unity of Word and sacrament – and hopefully this person will also be equipped to explain what the Eucharist means, and to help and encourage people to follow through in their lives the commitment they make when they feast with the Lord.

This *listening to the Host at his feast* is important

for all of us, but particularly when we come burdened with heavy worries and needs. For centuries, Anglican Christians listened to the words of Jesus used as an invitation to the table: 'Come to me, all who struggle and who are weighed down by a heavy load, and I will refresh you' (Matt. 11:28). He may call us to go on bearing the load, but he will certainly refresh us and give us new strength for it, if we will listen to him in Word and sacrament. But this means opening ourselves up to him. If we stay closed up, burdened and bound up with our worries, then we will be like the dinner-guest who hogs the limelight and leaves untouched by real *friendship* with the others present.

# 12. Paying attention to your fellow-guests

We saw in Part Two how fundamental this is. It is not just that we need to be at *peace* with our fellow-believers (the teaching of Paul), but that this meal expresses and celebrates *our very existence* as the people of Christ. The Passover helped Israelites to celebrate their origin as the people who together came out of Egypt. Jesus took the Passover and told his disciples to use it to celebrate *him*, not the Exodus. So just as the Exodus gave rise to the people of God of the *old* covenant, Jesus by his death creates the people of God of the *new* covenant. So in the Eucharist we celebrate what *we are*, as well as what *he is*. He is our Head, we are his body.

When we looked at Paul's teaching in 1 Corinthians 11, I only commented briefly on the way in which chapter 11 leads into chapter 12. Having taught the Corinthians about 'the body of Christ' in the Eucharist, Paul goes on to teach them about the 'one body' which they are, in Christ. They need to overcome their divisions and learn to serve one another, employing the variety of 'gifts', 'ministries' and 'powers' which 'the one Spirit distributes to each and every one of us, just as he wishes' (1 Cor. 12:4-11). For 'just as our physical body is a single unit, but has many parts, and all the parts of the body, though many, yet make up one body, *so it is with Christ*' (1 Cor. 12:12).

At the Eucharist we need to 'discern the body' in both senses (1 Cor. 11:29): Jesus' body as present in the 'signs' of bread and wine, and his body as present in the church around us.

Many traditions, sadly, still celebrate the Eucharist in a way which focuses on each individual worshipper, rather than on the *occasion* which draws us together. This is largely a result of the individualistic ethos of our western culture. I have led countless early morning Communions at which I was the only one who spoke, and people barely exchanged a word with each other either before or after the service. They were beautiful, quiet occasions of fellowship with the Lord ... but hardly with each other. Aesthetically very pleasing, very English, very reserved, very individualistic, very far from St Paul.

Even traditions very different from this Anglican one can yet have the same individual focus at the Eucharist. Pentecostalism is much less reserved, and yet (as one Pentecostal leader tells me), the style of celebrating the Eucharist usually lays emphasis on the private, individual relationship between each believer and the Lord.

We cannot help being children of our own culture, of course. I am a reserved Englishman, whether I like it or not (though with a welcome dash of Irish romance! I try to keep it hidden). But sometimes our culture can be an obstacle to spiritual growth, and we need to resist its effects. I think this is one such case. If emotional reserve (which is not in itself a bad thing) produces *social isolation*, we must recognise that this is not what God wants for us, and take steps to improve the situation.

Sometimes I wish I were a demonstrative Latin! But all cultures have their own difficulties, and for all of us the fundamental challenge is not actually to be *demonstrative* with others, but to be *loving*. It is genuine, heartfelt, unaffected Christian *love* which builds fellowship – and which in any case is at the heart of the Eucharist. We come to the Lord's table because we love him, in response to his great love for us. Gently then, let us begin to love the others who are our fellow-guests at the meal.

There are many ways in which we can draw out and encourage this aspect of our 'enjoyment':

(1) *Pray for others during the service*. I greatly enjoy doing this. If you belong to a church where people move forward to receive communion at the front, why not quietly pray for each person in turn as they get up or return? Pray with love and imagination. Pray particularly for the people in front of you, or on either side, when you yourself receive communion. Presbyterian churches often retain the

practice of actually sitting at specially prepared tables to receive communion: what a wonderful opportunity to pray for the others sitting at the table with you.

(2) *Don't dash off at the end.* The time after the service is part of the worship – or can be, if it continues to celebrate 'fellowship'. This is a chance to show your concern for people and to find out about their needs – perhaps to follow up thoughts that came to you as you prayed for people during the service. If your church does not yet encourage people to stay by serving coffee and biscuits, why not take the initiative and offer to organise this?

Some churches start at the other end, and serve refreshments before the service. One church I know produces coffee and hot doughnuts half an hour before the service begins! Anything that encourages and enables us to feast *together* with the Lord is helpful.

(3) *Make the most of 'The Peace'*, if your church follows this practice. The modern services all tend to include this moment of open fellowship. Initially many (British!) worshippers found it hard to cope with: it was hard to overcome reserve and wish 'the peace of the Lord' to complete strangers in surrounding pews.

But this was not a bright idea cooked up by the compilers of the new services. It is one of the most ancient features of the Eucharist, and goes back at least to the second century. Writing around 135 AD,

Justin Martyr tells us that, at the Eucharist, between the prayers and the thanksgiving over the bread and wine, 'we greet one another with a kiss'. From this point onward, 'the kiss of peace' was a regular feature of the Eucharist. It is a pity that the practice was dropped, because it expresses a vital truth: our *unity* at the table is crucial! Without it, there cannot be unity with the Lord.

'The Peace' is a lovely opportunity to give a warm expression of Christian love and fellowship to those around us. Some churches turn into a rugby scrum at this point, and spend five or ten minutes milling around greeting each other. Great!

(4) *Take opportunities for deeper sharing of needs and prayer*. Many churches, especially those with a 'charismatic' emphasis, offer an opportunity for deeper ministry at the Eucharist. Sometimes people are invited to stay at the communion-rail if they would like to share needs and pray with someone. Sometimes there is a team of people ready to pray with folk after the service.

If we come to the Eucharist burdened with particular worries (see the comments above), then it must be good to share them, if possible, with fellow-believers as well as with the Lord. Sometimes they may be too difficult and personal to share in detail – but even in such cases it would be good to share the sense of pain with someone else, so that they can pray for us. A good time of fellowship over coffee after the service can give informal opportunities for prayer with people like this.

There is one woman in our church who is great at this. Several people have said to me, 'I was chatting to Rose after the service, and suddenly she said, "Why don't we pray together about that?" So she prayed right there, in the middle of the room! It was wonderful! I've never prayed like that before!' Rose has taught me a lot about keeping both the directions of fellowship going together – the vertical dimension (with the Lord) and the horizontal (with each other).

Maybe Rose is helped by the fact that she is Kenyan. Many African Christians seem to have a spontaneous warmth and outgoing concern which comes harder to Anglo-Saxons and northern Europeans! But no, this is not Africa speaking. It is Rose's love for the Lord and for his children which leads her to minister in that way, *paying close attention to her fellow-guests*.

# 13. Thinking of others not there

It is a staggering thought: whenever we celebrate the Eucharist, there are literally *millions* of other churches throughout the world doing the same thing at more or less the same time. In every nation, in hundreds of different languages, under every conceivable political regime, in huge cathedrals and tiny chapels, in the open air, in *favelas* and front rooms and converted cinemas, with great pomp and with spontaneous dancing, with the dignity of tradition and under the inspiration of the Spirit, with five present and with five thousand ... *all the time* this wonderful Feast is celebrated.

If the Eucharist is all about *fellowship*, what are we to say about our relationship with these millions of others who feast, like us, in remembrance of Jesus? In some sense we must remember the *worldwide* fellowship to which we are joined by our common membership of the body of Christ. And of course that fellowship extends through time as well as space: celebrating this meal brings us into a vast company of all those who have worshipped in this way over nearly twenty centuries. We are not alone! In fact there are several ways in which *the walls around our Feast should be transparent*:

(1) *We remember our family tree*. The attitudes to *tradition* vary enormously in different parts of the Christian church. Some are happy just to think of themselves as prolonging the nourishing traditions of the past. Others are deeply suspicious of tradition because it could quench the spontaneity of the Spirit. Others again cherish a particular tradition which they believe has rescued the truth from the clutches of error in the rest of the church.

I do not want to get involved in the debates which this throws up! I simply want to say: we cannot do justice to the *fellowship* to which the Eucharist points us, if we ignore our family tree and our fathers and mothers in the faith – whatever tradition we want to identify with. The body of Christ is much bigger than our local church, and we are one with our forebears who left us the heritage that has nurtured us. Usually, this aspect of the Eucharist is expressed in the form and content of the service itself. Each church follows its own traditions and thus expresses its family identity. Don't forget the time-line to which you belong.

I find *saying the Creed* moving, from this point of view. The 'Nicene' Creed has been used at the Eucharist ever since it was written by the Council of Bishops at Nicea in 325 AD – representing the whole church at that time. It crosses all the subsequent divisions of the church – first the division between the Catholic and Orthodox churches, and then the division between the Catholic and Protestant churches at the Reformation. I am so glad that many modern services retain the Nicene Creed.

In fact, if your church uses a printed form of service for the Eucharist, it will almost certainly have much in common with the other forms of service developed in other churches over the last thirty years. And one of the factors that has guided the recent revision of the services was a desire to recover the most ancient forms. There are many detailed differences between the services used by Catholics, Orthodox, Anglicans, Episcopalians, Methodists, Baptists and United Reformed, but they have one thing in common: the general *shape* of the service goes right back to the earliest of which we know. Around the year 215 AD, a man named Hippolytus recorded the form of service used for the Eucharist in Rome – which, he tells us, had already been in use there for some time.

According to Hippolytus the service had this shape:

 * *The kiss of peace* (though this was not the first thing: Hippolytus was describing a Eucharist after the consecration of a bishop)
 * *The presentation of the bread and wine* (they are brought to the bishop)
 * The so-called *Sursum Corda*, which went like this:

Bishop: The Lord be with you!
Everyone: And with your spirit!
Bishop: Up with your hearts!
Everyone: We have them with the Lord.
Bishop: Let us give thanks to the Lord!
Everyone: It is fitting and right.

\*The *Thanksgiving*, which began by thanking God for giving his Son to be our Saviour, described Jesus' words and actions at the Last Supper, and finally offered the bread and cup to God, praying that he would send his Holy Spirit to unite us in praise of him through Christ. I have given this prayer in the final chapter.

This may look quite familiar to you! If your service follows this pattern, then you stand in a living tradition with all who have feasted *in this way*.

But the *form* of the service is not nearly so important (so Paul would tell us) as its *substance*. And simply in obeying the command, 'Do this in remembrance of me', we bind ourselves to all who have similarly obeyed it, however different from us they were in other ways.

(2) *We think about our living relatives*. This is even more important. Do our Eucharists have a worldwide feel to them? They ought to, if possible. The time of prayer is crucial here. We can bring the pain and mission of the church worldwide to God

– perhaps focusing on one or two particular needs of special concern. Does your church have a 'missionary secretary' or 'prayer co-ordinator' whose job it is to inspire concern for the needs of the church elsewhere? This is always important, but especially at the Eucharist.

(3) *We share the pain of the world.* This point underlies the last one. In the Eucharist we celebrate the love of one who gave himself for a lost world. At the Eucharist, therefore, it is appropriate to – no, we *must* – bear the needs of that lost world on our own hearts as we come before him. As we do this, we will be sharing his pain, just in a tiny way – the agony he felt before the cross, as the sin and death of the world pressed in upon him.

We need to be careful about this. We will be totally overwhelmed if we try to take all the woe of the world upon ourselves in prayer at the Eucharist. The point is, *he* bears it – praise him! So we don't have to shoulder it ourselves. But we will not 'enjoy' real fellowship with him, if we come to his table *heedless* of the compassion for a suffering and sinful world which took him to the cross.

In the Catholic tradition it has been customary to 'say a Mass' for a *particular* need. I have always been a little suspicious of this practice, because it seemed to attach a magical significance to the Eucharist. But maybe I was misunderstanding it. It is certainly right to *bring the needs of those he loves before the Lord in prayer*, and at no time is it more appropriate to do that than when we celebrate his sacrifice for the world, and remind ourselves of our fellowship with all his children worldwide – *thinking of others not there.*

# 14. Eating the meal

Yes, when we go out for a meal we enjoy the company of our friends, the surroundings, the atmosphere, the music, the conversation – but actually the basic purpose is *food*. The other things are good, but this is essential: unless we eat, we die. So far we have been thinking about all the 'other things' in the Eucharist. Now we need to focus on the action at the heart of it all, the thing that Jesus chiefly had in mind as he broke the bread and gave the cup: he wanted his disciples to *eat* and *drink* in remembrance of him. How may we do this well?

I am not going to refer to the 'nuts and bolts' of doing it – whether it is better to receive communion in your seat or at an altar rail, whether you should stand or kneel, whether there should be music or not, whether children should be allowed to receive or not; nor am I going to discuss the words that are used, nor whether it is better to use bread or wafers, alcoholic or non-alcoholic wine ... all these issues are matters of local practice, and just two things are important: (a) you need to be happy to accept what happens in your church (even if you don't personally like this or that), and (b) you need to know what to do. The occasion will be spoilt for you if you are worried about where to go, or what to do with your hands, or when to eat the bread. I will touch on a few practical matters in the next chapter. But in this chapter, I focus on the actual feasting which makes this meal a meal. There are five things, I believe, which will enable us to receive what the Lord wants to give us in the Eucharist:

*(1) Be clear about its meaning*
This helps a great deal, and I hope that this book may have been useful in this respect. But *even if you disagree with this book*, and understand the Eucharist differently, it is still important (because it will be helpful to you) to be as clear as you can about what it means, and what you are doing by participating. What I write in this chapter does not depend very closely on the understanding of the Eucharist I suggested in Part Two, so I hope you will be able to benefit from the suggestions here, whatever your view of it.

At rock bottom, of course, all the churches agree that in the Eucharist we are obeying the command of the Lord to remember his death for us, and that to eat and drink in this way is a wonderful expression of Christian faith. The various interpretations simply involve further thoughts and explanations, added to this 'core'. Try to be as clear in your own mind about it all. Get your minister / pastor / priest / elder to explain if necessary!

*(2) Bring the whole of you to the Lord*

This may seem a little strange. The point is this: we are not just 'souls' or 'spirits', but *bodies* as well. Many people think of communion as a 'spiritual' event, something that will do us good deep inside, as we meet the Lord 'spiritually'. This is true, but it is only half the truth. I can clarify this point by asking, What is the spiritual problem from which, above all, we want to be saved by Christ? The answer is: *death*. But death is a *physical* problem, first and foremost! *and* a spiritual problem. We need the touch of a Saviour in both halves of our make-up, physical and spiritual.

And that, of course, is what he came to do for us. If the human race needed nothing more than a bit of *spiritual* renovation, God could have sent a *spirit* to do that. But sin has affected our whole nature, both spiritual and physical. The physical weakness and death which afflicts us human beings is all part of our problem – in fact, it is the result of our alienation from God, the source of all life. So we need a Saviour who matches our need. And we have one, in the Son of God who *became flesh* for us (John 1:14), and who shares our humanity to the extent of *dying* with us, and for us.

That is why it is so wonderful that we have *physical* symbols of Christ to consume at the Eucharist. The bread and wine are *flesh*, part of the stuff of this world, just as he was, and just as we are. He does not just deal with some vague spiritual malaise, but addresses our death – in fact takes our death upon him, so that we may receive his life. The words of administration in the old Anglican *Book of Common Prayer* brought this out nicely: 'The Body of our Lord Jesus Christ, which was given for thee, preserve thy body and soul unto everlasting life'. I am sad that this emphasis has disappeared with modern revision.

So: bring your *whole* self to him. You are a physical being, and he is interested in enabling you to 'glorify God in your body', as Paul urges the Corinthians (1 Cor. 6:20). Come to him with the whole range of your need – physical, emotional, moral, spiritual.

Ask him for physical healing, if that is your need. Remember that Jesus' way is generally deliverance *through* suffering, rather than deliverance *from* it – isn't that what the symbols loudly say? So even if his will is not your healing, you may be sure that he will give you the strength and courage to bear whatever pain you face. Ask him for that, too.

Bring your sexuality to him. That is a powerful part of your physical make-up, whether you are married or not. You do not leave it at the church door. It needs to be brought to Christ, deliberately and regularly, and offered to him for healing and sanctifying.

Ask him for emotional wholeness, if that is your need. In bereavement look to him for comfort, and hear a word of assurance from one whose body was torn apart, but who lives for evermore. Afflicted with depression, just focus on the elements (the bread and wine), and let them speak to you of one who understands, and is with you. If you have been torn by abuse, let the elements remind you of one who experienced dreadful physical abuse at the hands of evil men, but who died with a prayer for his abusers on his lips. Such love! Whatever your need, bring it to him honestly, and trustingly, and prayerfully – and, if possible, not secretly. Share it with someone you trust, so that the *fellowship* will be not just vertical, but horizontal also.

And ask him for forgiveness. *Don't* fall into the trap of thinking that sin keeps you away! The bread and wine are God's gift for sinners, who have made a mess of their lives and others'. They point us to one who *wants* to forgive us so much that he died to win that possibility. All that stops him from giving it, is our unwillingness to receive it. Come gladly with your sin! One of the wonderful things about Jesus was that, although he was so holy himself, the most awful sinners actually felt *attracted* to him, not repelled. Prostitutes and reprobates *wanted* to be with him, because they felt accepted and cleansed by his presence. He is still the same. At his table, we can experience his presence still, and know that forgiveness which he alone can give.

*(3) Surrender to his power*

To eat the bread and the wine with faith is to act upon the promise of God: receive these as a sign of Christ, and you will live. The act of eating in itself, therefore, becomes part of the sign for us, when we do it in joyful faith. Here's how it works:

Eating is a powerful expression of trust. Every time I eat something, I surrender myself to it. If it is poisonous, it will damage me. I eat in faith that it is not poisonous, and that it will live up to its promise and nourish me well. I trust my wife. I know she does not want to poison me by her cooking. But eating is still a hazardous thing to do, however well-known the cook is! Food actually becomes part of me – that is why it can both nourish me and harm me. I absorb it into myself, and it feeds (or destroys) my tissues.

This is a powerful picture! When we eat the bread and wine, we *surrender ourselves to Christ, and express our desire that he should become part of the very fibre of our being*. We know that he will do us no harm – far from it. We want his power and love – his *Spirit* – to soak into us, body and soul, and to nourish us for the eternal life that starts tomorrow morning!

I find this a most helpful thought to bear in mind as I actually eat and swallow the bread and wine. I cannot go back. I have committed myself. I don't *want* to go back! Christ I gladly welcome into my heart, my life, my body, to seep through me, cleanse me and nourish me with the life-giving power of his love.

*(4) Look forward to the resurrection*

'As often as you eat this bread and drink the cup, you proclaim the death of the Lord until he comes' (1 Cor. 11:26). We looked briefly at this verse in chapter 8. It fits in here because of the thought about our *death* above. In the Eucharist (as indeed in baptism) we face seriously and openly the fact of our coming death. This is not morbid. It is *realistic*. We do not flee from death, we accept it as the inevitable end of our existence on this earth.

But it is horrible, nonetheless. Death is an *enemy*. The 'last enemy', says Paul (1 Cor. 15:26). It is an enemy because *it totally destroys our bodies*. If we want to think in a biblical way about ourselves, then we have to say that our bodies are not a detachable part of the real 'us'. The real you and I is not some immaterial or unbodily bit inside (a 'soul') which can live just as well without a body as with one. If the bank where I keep my money burns down, it is no great problem for *the bank*. The bank itself, as an institution, remains unaffected. It can simply move to new premises. But we are not like that. Suppose, instead, that a *library* burns down, including all its books. How can a library continue to exist without its books?

That is why the Bible pictures death as something horrible, which strikes at our very being. We are like that library, which depends totally upon its physical make-up for its existence. One day we will experience that kind of destruction! *But* ... in Christ death has been overcome. He died like no-one else, because his death led to life. So, when we eat these symbols of his death, we are lining ours up with his, in faith: we are acting on the promise, 'Whoever eats my flesh and drinks my blood has eternal life, and I will raise that person up, on the last day' (John 6:54). We are saying that we want *our* death to be *his* death, so that we, like him, may rise to eternal life.

Our western culture has sanitised death out of our everyday awareness. But we are the first age which has managed to do this. Other cultures were (and are) much more realistic about death. We have achieved this by a huge act of self-deception. By our adverts, our music, our 'life insurance', our health-care systems, our cult of youth, our New Age 'anything's possible' philosophy, and our determination to live for today and forget tomorrow, our culture has managed to defeat death, it thinks. But we Christians know better. Even if they call us morbid, we will refuse to be taken in by this soul-destroying clap-trap. We will be realistic, even if no-one else is. And at the Eucharist, at the very moment where the world thinks we have retreated into mumbo-jumbo and make-believe, we face up to the fact of death, embrace it as part of our humanity, and absorb into ourselves the symbols of one man's death – the only man who has truly defeated death and offers that victory to us.

The death of Christ, Paul tells us, is to be our theme-song 'until he comes'. The Eucharist looks forward to the final defeat of death and evil, and the coming of the new heaven and new earth in which Jesus our Lord will reign for evermore, and we will 'feast' with him. The Eucharist is a signpost which points in two directions, as we have seen – back to the cross, and forward to glory. Because of the cross, we have 'the hope of glory' (Rom. 5:2, Col. 1:27). Partaking in the Eucharist expresses our faith in that hope, and *assures* us, on God's authority, that our faith is not in vain.

What will it be like in heaven? What are we looking forward to? The Bible does not describe it. It just uses some pictures to convey a feel of it. And one of these is feasting: see Matthew 8:11; 22:1-14; Luke 12:35-38; 22:30; Revelation 2:17; 19:9. So 'Feasting with the Lord' can be a description of heaven, as well as of the Eucharist. In the Eucharist, we sample a little of heaven in advance. There too, we will be *enjoying his company; enjoying each other's company; celebrating what he has done to get us there; and expressing our 100% commitment to him – with great joy.*

### (5) Be thankful

The last point is the simplest, but also the most important. The word 'Eucharist' actually means

'thanksgiving', and so it cannot be what it is meant
to be, unless we eat and drink with thankfulness.

For Paul, failure to thank God was one of the
chief things wrong with the world – one of the first
fruits of its fallenness. Describing fallen humankind in Romans 1:21 he writes, 'though they knew
God, they did not glorify him as God or give thanks
to him, and so trivialised themselves in all their
thinking as their minds and hearts were darkened'.
I like the translation 'trivialised themselves' here:
it is Eugene Peterson's suggestion in his new translation of the New Testament, *The Message*
(Navpress, 1993). When we fail to give thanks to
God, we lose contact with one of the deepest roots
of our being and become *trivialised*, living purely
on the level of earthly cares and joys.

The Eucharist points us in the opposite direction
completely. Here we celebrate the deepest root of
our being in God, through Christ, and by *giving
thanks* for who he is, and for all he has done for us,
we set our earthly cares and joys in their right
perspective. We belong to him totally, and receive
everything as from his hand, and trust him absolutely, and thank him as children with their Father
– even if he has called us to live what the world
around would call a bleak and 'thankless' life.
Whatever our circumstances or our trials, the Eucharist says to us, 'Nothing can separate us from the
love of God in Christ Jesus our Lord!' (Romans
8:39), and encourages us 'to give thanks to our God

and Father at all times, and for all people, in the name of our Lord Jesus Christ!' (Ephesians 5:20).

So make sure that *thankfulness* is the dominant note in your mind. Why not have your own special prayer of thanksgiving to say as you return from the Communion rail, or in the few quiet moments that follow eating and drinking? In this way it will really be a *Eucharistic* feast for you!

# 15. Some practical issues

In this final chapter I will pick up some practical questions which people ask, some of them things which have been deliberately left aside in previous chapters.

*(1) Should I partake if I am ill? And what about the spread of serious infections through the cup, like HIV?*
The appearance of HIV and AIDS has caused all churches to think about the possible dangers of using a common cup. How real are these dangers? Some have suggested that alcoholic wine reduces the risk of infection, especially if a silver cup is used, but that non-alcoholic wine used in a common cup is dangerous. Is this true?

Scientific studies have been carried out to answer these questions. *The Journal of Infection* published a study in 1988 (vol. 16, pp 3-23) by Noel Gill of the Public Health Laboratory in London, entitled 'The hazard of infection from the shared communion cup'. This is a very detailed study which looks at the possibility of the transfer of infections of many sorts through the communion cup, including HIV. Only some contagious diseases are transmitted through saliva, and obviously it is these which might cause particular concern. The author draws on a range of experiments and studies conducted by others, and these are his conclusions:

* Bacteria can indeed be transferred from mouth to mouth by use of a common cup. However, 'no episode of disease attributable to the shared communion cup has ever been reported'.

* Bacteria are indeed killed off by the alcohol in the wine, but it takes several minutes for this to take effect. The alcohol has no immediate effect, and therefore there is no practical difference between alcoholic and non-alcoholic wine.

* A silver cup also has a slight sterilising effect, but the same observation applies.

* Wiping the lip of the cup with a cloth between communicants is very helpful in reducing the risk of the transfer of infection.

* The HIV virus is only infrequently present in the saliva of people with HIV and AIDS, and there is only one report of the possible transmission of HIV through exchange of saliva (in intimate kissing). The likelihood of the *indirect* transmission of HIV – on the rim of a cup – is very low indeed.

We may thank God that it seems to be very difficult indeed to become infected with HIV: mainly through direct sexual contact. However, the possibility of passing on other infections which are typically transmitted through saliva – particularly mumps, and herpes (cold-sores) – makes it advisable to be careful. If there are susceptible people in the church, particularly elderly folk, then they may be at risk (a) if someone with a bad cold drinks next to them, and (b) the cup is passed to them unwiped. But actually they are *more* at risk if someone sneezes over them!

If you have a cold-sore on your mouth, it would be best not to participate, or to do so last. If you are in any doubt at all, have a word with your minister or priest about it. The demands of fellowship must come first.

*(2) Does it matter if for some reason I cannot actually receive the bread or wine?*
You might abstain voluntarily (see the last point), or you might have a physical condition, temporary or permanent, which makes it impossible to participate. Don't worry – God understands! Which is more important: to be *part* of the body of Christ, or to *feed symbolically* on the body of Christ? St Paul would not hesitate: belonging is more important! The vital thing is to belong to a fellowship which is in living communion with the Lord, and to be living close to him yourself in prayer.

If you have to observe a gluten-free diet, it is worth knowing that gluten-free wafers are available for use in communion. They can be obtained from Faith House Bookshop, 7 Tufton Street, London SW1P 3QN (telephone 0171 222 6952).

*(3) I have a problem with alcoholism: should I avoid alcoholic communion wine, or doesn't it matter?*
Yes, you should avoid it. There is no case where it has been proved that drinking the wine at Communion has caused an alcoholic to relapse into drinking. But this does not mean that there is no danger. And in any case, you will not be able to concentrate on what the Eucharist means for you, if you are thinking about the alcohol in the wine. Organisations that seek to help alcoholics recommend abstaining from alcoholic communion wine.

Have a word with your minister or priest. Some churches use two cups, one with alcoholic and one with non-alcoholic wine. If necessary, you can be sure that the blessing of the Eucharist is not reduced if you only take the bread!

*(4) Is it all right if our house-group decides to have a simple Eucharist together?*
At the beginning, all Eucharists took place in this kind of setting (Acts 2:46). If you have developed a close sense of fellowship in your house-group, then it can be very special to 'break bread' together in this way.

But you will need to fit in with the custom of your church, whatever it is. Some churches will expect house-groups to do this under their own steam, and whenever they wish. Other churches will expect the minister or priest to be invited to come and lead it – or at the least to be asked or told about it. Other churches will feel that it is inappropriate, and that the Eucharist should only be celebrated on central occasions. Make sure that you do not offend the wider fellowship for the sake of the fellowship in your group.

*(5) Can I take Communion when visiting another church?*

This question often arises when on holiday. Obviously, if you belong to a large denomination, then there will be no problem about taking Communion at another church of your denomination. But holidays give an excellent opportunity to experience what happens in other churches of a different type. You might find yourself at a Communion service.

If this happens, then it is worth remembering that Anglican, Episcopalian, Methodist and United Reformed churches, and most Baptist churches, are happy to admit to Communion all who are regular communicants in their own church. This 'open' approach allows some wonderful expressions of fellowship across denominational boundaries.

Some Baptist churches and Brethren fellowships operate a 'members only' policy, although they might be willing to allow you to participate if you are able to chat to the minister or elder about it beforehand. Catholic and Orthodox churches similarly make admittance to Communion a sign of commitment to their own church, and so do not generally allow casual participation by visitors.

You can feel something of the pain of Jesus himself at the division of his church, if you have to sit and watch a 'fellowship in the body of Christ' (1 Cor. 10:16) from which you yourself are excluded.

Strictly speaking, Catholic churches do not permit their members to participate in Eucharists at other churches, even where there is an open invitation to do so. But at the same time they are often prepared to allow considerable freedom of conscience in these matters.

# 16. A selection of Communion Hymns

Communion services often provide quiet moments for reflection and prayer, particularly while the bread and wine are being administered. These moments can be used in different ways – in quiet prayer for others around, or for our own particular needs, or in reading the Bible (perhaps a Psalm, or the passage on which the sermon was based), or in using other prayers or hymns to express our worship. There are some beautiful Communion hymns from various traditions, and in order to provide a resource for such quiet moments, some of the best are given here.

*This hymn was written by Horatius Bonar, a Scottish Presbyterian minister, for a Communion at Greenock in October 1855. I think this is one of my favourites of all:*

Here, O my Lord, I see thee face to face;
Here would I touch and handle things unseen,
Here grasp with firmer hand the eternal grace,
And all my weariness upon thee lean.

Here would I feed upon the bread of God,
Here drink with thee the royal wine of heaven;
Here would I lay aside each earthy load,
Here taste afresh the calm of sin forgiven.

This is the hour of banquet and of song,
This is the heavenly table spread for me;
Here let me feast, and feasting, still prolong
The brief, bright hour of fellowship with thee.

Too soon we rise; the symbols disappear;
The feast, though not the love, is past and gone;
The bread and wine remove, but thou art here,
Nearer than ever, still my Shield and Sun.

I have no help but thine; nor do I need
Another arm save thine to rest upon;
It is enough, my Lord, enough indeed;
My strength is in thy might, thy might alone.

I have no wisdom, save in him who is
My Wisdom and my Teacher, both in one;
No wisdom can I lack while thou art wise,
No teaching do I crave save thine alone.

Mine is the sin, but thine the righteousness;
Mine is the guilt, but thine the cleansing blood;
Here is my robe, my refuge, and my peace –
Thy blood, thy righteousness, O Lord my God.

I know that deadly evils compass me;
Dark perils threaten, yet I would not fear,
Nor poorly shrink, nor feebly turn to flee;
Thou, O my Christ, art Buckler, Sword, and Spear.

But see, the Pillar-cloud is rising now,
And moving onward through the desert night;
It beckons, and I follow, for I know
It leads me to the heritage of light.

Feast after feast thus comes and passes by,
Yet, passing, points to the glad feast above,
Giving sweet foretaste of the festal joy,
The Lamb's great bridal feast of bliss and love.

*Another hymn by Horatius Bonar, published in a collection
of his Communion hymns in 1881:*

On merit not my own I stand;
On doings which I have not done,
Merit beyond what I can claim,
Doings more perfect than my own.

Upon a life I have not lived,
Upon a death I did not die,
Another's life, Another's death,
I stake my whole eternity.

Not on the tears which I have shed:
Not on the sorrows I have known,
Another's tears, Another's griefs,
On them I rest, on them alone.

Jesus, O Son of God, I build
On what thy cross has done for me;
There both my death and life I read,
My guilt, my pardon there I see.

Lord, I believe; oh deal with me
As one who has thy Word believed!
I take the gift, Lord look on me
As one who has thy gift received.

I taste the love the gift contains,
I clasp the pardon which it brings,
And pass up to the living source
Above, whence all this fulness springs.

Here at thy feast, I grasp the pledge
Which life eternal to me seals,
Here in the bread and wine I read
The grace and peace thy death reveals.

O fulness of the eternal grace,
O wonders past all wondering!
Here in the hall of love and song,
We sing the praises of our King.

*This beautiful poem by George Herbert (1593-1633) is an encouragement to all who feel they are not worthy:*

Love bade me welcome; yet my soul drew back,
    Guilty of dust and sin.
But quick-eyed Love, observing me grow slack,
    From my first entrance in,
Drew nearer to me, sweetly questioning,
    If I lacked anything.

A guest, I answered, worthy to be here:
    Love said, You shall be he.
I, the unkind, ungrateful? Ah, my dear,
    I cannot look on thee.
Love took my hand, and smiling did reply,
    Who made the eyes but I?

Truth, Lord, but I have marred them: let my shame
    Go where it doth deserve.

And know you not, says Love, who bore the blame?
    My dear, then I will serve!
You must sit down, says Love, and taste my meat:
    So I did sit, and eat.

*Charles Wesley wrote no fewer than 166 Communion
hymns, an output which illustrates the emphasis placed by
the early Methodists on the Lord's Supper. Here are three
of his best:*

Jesus, we thus obey
Thy last and kindest Word;
Here, in thine own appointed way,
We come to meet thee, Lord.

Our hearts we open wide,
To make the Saviour room;
And lo! the Lamb, the Crucified,
The sinner's Friend, is come.

Thy presence makes the feast;
Now let our spirits feel
The glory not to be expressed,
The joy unspeakable.

With high and heavenly bliss
Thou dost our spirits cheer;
Thy house of banqueting is this,
And thou hast brought us here.

Now let our souls be fed
With manna from above,
And over us thy banner spread
Of everlasting love.

*Charles Wesley understood the Eucharist in a powerful
way, as illustrated by this hymn-prayer:*

Come, Holy Ghost, thine influence shed,
And realise the sign;
Thy life infuse into the bread,
Thy power into the wine.

Effectual let the tokens prove
And made, by heavenly art,
Fit channels to convey thy love
To every faithful heart.

Now on the sacred table laid,
Christ's flesh becomes our food;
His life is to our souls conveyed
In sacramental blood.

Blest be the Lord, for ever blest,
Who bought us with a price,
And bids his ransomed servants feast
On his great sacrifice.


*Another beautiful Wesley hymn:*

Victim divine, thy grace we claim,
While thus thy precious death we show:
Once offered up, a spotless Lamb,
In thy great temple here below,
Thou didst for all mankind atone
And standest now before the throne.

Thou standest in the holy place,
As now for guilty sinners slain;
The blood of sprinkling speaks, and prays,
All prevalent for helpless man;
Thy blood is still our ransom found,
And speaks salvation all around.

We need not now go up to heaven
To bring the long-sought Saviour down;
Thou art to all already given,
Thou dost ev'n now thy banquet crown;
To every faithful soul appear,
And show thy real presence here!

*Reginald Heber was the bishop of Calcutta in the 1820s.*
*This little gem is one of his best known hymns:*

Bread of the world in mercy broken,
Wine of the soul in mercy shed,
By whom the words of life were spoken,
And in whose death our sins are dead.

Look on the heart by sorrow broken,
Look on the tears by sinners shed,
And make your feast to us the token
That by your grace our souls are fed.

*There now follows a selection of hymns of modern origin.*
*This first one is by Michael Saward:*

'Peace be with you all', we sing;
peace from Christ, our lord and king;
he it is who makes us one,
God's eternal rising Son.

Bound together in his name,
welded by the Spirit's flame,
at his table here we kneel
and his living presence feel.

Bread is broken for our food;
wine we share in gratitude.
His the flesh and blood he gave
for the world he died to save.

So with empty hands, we bow
to receive our Saviour now
and, renewed in mind and heart
in the peace of Christ depart.

*(Copyright Michael Saward / Jubilate Hymns)*

*By Robert Stamps:*

O welcome, all ye noble saints of old,
As now before your very eyes unfold
The wonders all so long ago foretold:
God and man at table are sat down!

Elders, martyrs, all are falling down
And prophets, patriarchs are gathering round;
What angels longed to see, now man has found.
God and man at table are sat down!

Beggars, lame and harlots also here,
Repentant publicans are drawing near,
Wayward sons come home without a fear:
God and man at table are sat down!

Who is this who spreads the victory feast?
Who is this who makes our warring cease?
Jesus, risen Saviour, Prince of Peace.
God and man at table are sat down!

Here he gives himself to us as bread,
Here, as wine, we drink the blood he shed.
Born to die, we eat and live instead.
God and man at table are sat down!

Worship in the presence of the Lord,
With joyful songs and hearts in one accord,
And let our host of table be adored:
God and man at table are sat down!

When at last this earth shall pass away,
When Jesus and his bride are one to stay,
The feast of love is just begun that day:
God and man at table are sat down!

*Graham Kendrick's hymns have brought great blessing to
many Christians. This little example is ideal for saying
slowly to yourself as you prepare for communion:*

Immanuel, O Immanuel,
Bowed in awe I worship at your feet,
And sing Immanuel, God is with us,
Sharing our humanness, our pain,
Feeling my weaknesses, my shame,
Taking the punishment, the blame,
Immanuel.

And now my words cannot explain
All that my heart cannot contain
How great are the glories of your name,
Immanuel!

*A hymn by Fred Kaan reflecting on the meaning of 'The Peace':*

Put peace into each others' hands,
And like a treasure hold it;
Protect it like a candle-flame,
With tenderness enfold it.

Put peace into each others' hands,
With loving expectation;
Be gentle in your words and ways,
In touch with God's creation.

Put peace into each others' hands,
Like bread we break for sharing;
Look people warmly in the eye:
Our life is meant for caring.

As at communion, shape your hands
Into a waiting cradle;
The gift of Christ receive, revere,
United round the table.

Put Christ into each others' hands,
He is love's deepest measure;

In love make peace, give peace a chance,
And share it like a treasure.

*A lovely hymn by Richard Gillard, movingly expressing the
commitment to each other which the Eucharist involves:*

Brother, sister, let me serve you,
Let me be as Christ to you;
Pray that I may have the grace to
Let you be my servant too.

We are pilgrims on a journey,
And companions on the road;
We are here to help each other
Walk the mile and bear the load.

I will hold the Christ-light for you
In the night-time of your fear;
I will hold my hand out to you,
Speak the peace you long to hear.

I will weep when you are weeping;
When you laugh I'll laugh with you;
I will share your joy and sorrow
Till we've seen this journey through.

When we sing to God in heaven
We shall find such harmony,
Born of all we've known together
Of Christ's love and agony.

Brother, sister, let me serve you,
Let me be as Christ to you;
Pray that I may have the grace to
Let you be my servant too.

*There now follow two hymns by Bishop Timothy Dudley-Smith, whose work will surely be sung 200 years from now, just as we still sing the hymns of Charles Wesley. His writing has a powerful visual quality. In this first one, we follow Jesus to the cross:*

A purple robe, a crown of thorn,
a reed in his right hand;
before the soldiers' spite and scorn
I see my Saviour stand.

He bears between the Roman guard
the weight of all our woe;
a stumbling figure bowed and scarred
I see my Saviour go.

Fast to the cross's spreading span,
high in the sunlit air,
all the unnumbered sins of man
I see my Saviour bear.

He hangs, by whom the world was made,
beneath the darkened sky;
the everlasting ransom paid,
I see my Saviour die.

He shares on high his Father's throne
who once in mercy came;
for all his love to sinners shown
I sing my Saviour's name.

*(Copyright 1968 Timothy Dudley-Smith)*

*This second hymn takes us straight to the upper room, and
we sit with the disciples:*

As in that upper room you left your seat
and took a towel and chose a servant's part,
so for today, Lord, wash again my feet,
who in your mercy died to cleanse my heart.

I bow before you, all my sin confessed,
to hear again the words of love you said;
and at your table, as your honoured guest,
I take and eat the true and living Bread.

So in remembrance of your life laid down
 I come to praise you for your grace divine;
saved by your cross, and subject to your crown,
strengthened for service by this bread and wine.

*(Copyright 1992 Timothy Dudley-Smith)*

*The following hymns are by my father, the Revd Alec
Motyer, and not previously published. I am grateful to him
for letting me include them here.*

   *The first was written for the congregation at Christ
Church, Westbourne, where he served from 1981 to 1989:
it is a meditation on the words of the Communion service
in the Anglican Book of Common Prayer, which describes*

*the death of Jesus as 'a full, perfect and sufficient sacrifice,*
*oblation and satisfaction for the sins of the whole world'.*

Come, stand and gaze upon the cross,
And marvel that on him were laid
Our sins, and trespasses, and guilt,
And *full* atonement there was made.

Consider him, the holy Christ,
The *perfect*, spotless, righteous one,
Who free from sin's accusing charge,
Bore all our sins as though his own.

From Calvary's darkness hear him cry
That all he came to do is done
For God's elect, a finished work,
*Sufficient* fully to atone.

Bow low before the Lamb of God,
Who took our place and paid our price;
The just who for the unjust died,
Their substitute, their *sacrifice*.

What mystery here! The Prince of life,
Immortal God, has freely died;
To God his *self-oblation* made,
And willingly was crucified!

Extol him now upon the throne,
At God's right hand, the church's Head.
Eternal justice *satisfied*!
He lives, he reigns, who once was dead.

*This hymn reflects on the story of the breakfast by the lake in John 21:*

Stand now as once upon the shore
You stood for that returning few;
Take knowledge of our weariness,
Our often failure and distress;
Call us, your children, back to you.

Lead us to your provision, Lord:
The food prepared, the table spread,
Abounding grace to meet our need,
Your flesh, your blood our food indeed,
O Prince of Life, the living bread.

Take in your nail-pierced hand of love
This covenant-pledge, this gracious sign;
Feed us who sit around your board,
Open our eyes to see you, Lord,
Through broken bread and poured out wine.

*This hymn meditates on the thought that signs of a death point to life:*

Emblems of suffering,
Means of his grace:
Jesus my Saviour
Died in my place.
Bread of affliction,
Wine of his pain,
Jesus is living,
Risen again.

Food all-sufficient,
Table well spread,
Bountiful Saviour,
Life-giving bread;
Wine of remembrance,
Sheltering blood,
Jesus is living,
True Lamb of God.

Bread that is broken,
Grace that is free:
Wounded my Saviour,
Healing for me.
Wine of forgiveness,
Blood to atone,
Jesus is living,
Christ on the throne.

Memories of Calvary,
Cross, nails and spear:
Sin-bearing Saviour,
Jesus is here.
Visions of glory,
Heaven restored,
Jesus is living,
Soon-coming Lord!

*This is the invitation to the Table used in the Prayer Book published by the Baptist Union of Great Britain in 1991:*

Come to this table, not because you must, but because you may, not because you are strong, but because you are weak;

Come, not because any goodness of your own gives you a right to come, but because you need mercy and help;

Come, because you love the Lord a little, and would like to love him more;

Come, because he loved you and gave himself for you;

Come and meet the risen Christ, for we are his body.

(Quoted from *Patterns and Prayers for Christian Worship* by permission of the Baptist Union of Great Britain)

*Here finally is the eucharistic prayer recorded by Hippolytus, the oldest Communion prayer we have. This was used in the church in Rome around the year 200:*

We render thanks to you, O God, through your beloved child Jesus Christ, whom in the last times you sent to us as Saviour and Redeemer and Angel of your will;

who is your inseparable Word, through whom you made all things, and in whom you are well pleased.

You sent him from heaven into the Virgin's womb; and, conceived in the womb, he was made flesh and was manifested as your Son, being born of the Holy Spirit and the Virgin.

Fulfilling your will and gaining for you a holy people, he stretched out his hands when he should suffer, that he might release from suffering those who have believed in you.

And when he was betrayed to voluntary suffering that he might destroy death, and break the bonds of the

devil, and tread down hell, and shine upon the righteous, and fix the limit, and manifest the resurrection,
he broke bread and gave thanks to you, saying, 'Take,
eat; this is my body, which shall be broken for you'.
Likewise also the cup, saying, 'This is my blood,
which is shed for you; when you do this, you make my
remembrance'.

Remembering therefore his death and resurrection, we offer to you the bread and the cup, giving you
thanks because you have held us worthy to stand
before you and minister to you.

And we ask that you would send your Holy Spirit
upon the offering of your holy church; that, gathering
them into one, you would grant to all who partake of
the holy things the fulness of the Holy Spirit, for the
confirmation of faith in truth;

that we may praise and glorify you through your
child Jesus Christ, through whom be glory and honour
to you, to the Father and the Son with the Holy Spirit,
in your holy church, both now and to the ages of ages.
Amen!

*After giving this prayer, Hippolytus comments that the
minister is encouraged to give thanks in his own words if he
wants to – but 'no one shall prevent him' if he decides to use
a fixed prayer like this. So we too may use the words and
prayers of others, and our own words also, as we come
before the Lord at his table.*

Steve Motyer lives in Watford, England, and works at London Bible College where he teaches New Testament. He is an Anglican minister, and has also taught at Oak Hill College, one of the theological colleges of the Church of England, and spent some years in pastoral ministry. He is married to Val, a social worker, and they have two sons and a daughter. He has written *Israel in the Plan of God* (IVP, 1989), *Unlock the Bible* (Scripture Union, 1992), *Ephesians* (Crossway Bible Guides, 1994), and *Men With A Message* (co-authored with John Stott, 1995). Currently he serves as an elder in a newly-planted church in Carpenders Park, the estate where he and his family live. He says that family life leaves little time spare time for hobbies, but that he finds playing the piano his chief source of relaxation.